WATFORD PAST

First published 2005
by Historical Publications Ltd
32 Ellington Street, London N7 8PL
(Tel: 020 7607 1628)

ISBN 1-905286-01-5
British Library Cataloguing-in-Publication Data
A catalogue record for this book is available from the British Library

Reproduction by Gilderson's, 31 Pitfield Street, London N1
Printed in Zaragoza, Spain by Edelvives

Acknowledgements

Without the help of the following people, writing this book would have been a far less enjoyable and enlightening experience.

Mary Forsyth for her unstinting support, assistance and time, for which I am extremely grateful. Sarah Priestley, Heritage Officer at the Watford Museum for her patience, and kindly offering me assistance with the section dealing with Watford Football Club, an area in which she proved enthusiastic and knowledgeable. I would also like to thank Sarah for taking me on a tour of Watford's listed buildings in the pouring rain with not a single word of complaint. Taj Mohammad, Museum Assistant, uncomplainingly tracked down my requested illustrations and kept me informed when he discovered others that he thought would be of interest. Marion Duffin, Arts & Heritage Manager at the Museum for her assistance, encouragement and advice, and Sonia Sagoo, Museum Administrator, who was never without a kind word. In addition to the Museum staff, the librarians in the Reference section of Watford's Central Library were unfailingly helpful. I would like to thank John Richardson for his guidance, and my wife Eleanor for her patience during my period of total Watford obsession. One thing that struck me in the writing of this book was the sense of pride of Watford's citizens in their past, and the strong sense of community that prevails.

The Illustrations

Illustrations have been reproduced with the kind permission of the following:
Paul Ailey: *39*
Robert Bard: *11, 16, 20, 22, 24, 25, 26, 29, 30, 31, 32, 33, 35, 38, 41, 46, 47, 48, 49, 50, 51, 53, 54, 56, 57, 58, 61, 62, 63, 64, 68, 71, 73, 74, 75, 77, 78, 81, 84, 85, 86, 87, 88, 90, 91, 92, 93, 95, 98, 100, 105, 115, 116, 119, 121, 122, 123, 124, 125, 126, 128, 133, 135, 138, 139, 140, 144*
J. Paul Getty Museum, Los Angeles: *43*
National Portrait Gallery: *40, 42*
St Mary's Church: *55*
Watford Grammar School for Boys: *72, 76*
Watford Museum: *2, 4, 5, 6, 7, 8, 9, 10, 13, 14, 15, 17, 18, 19, 21, 23, 36, 44, 60, 65, 70, 79, 82, 96, 97, 104, 106, 109, 110, 111, 112, 113, 114, 117, 118, 120, 130, 131, 132, 136, 137, 141, 142, 143*
www.watfordtheatre.co.uk *127*

Illustration 80 was taken from *Watford, a Pictorial Record* published in 1951
by the Festival of Britain Committee.

WATFORD PAST

Robert Bard

HISTORICAL PUBLICATIONS

Introduction

To most people, Watford is a sign on the M1 motorway, a football club previously associated with Elton John, or perhaps the first stop on the railway line from Euston to the north. The perception is of a suburb dominated by concrete and a lack of open space. The Harlequin shopping complex and the one-way road system have taken over the inner town and at first glance constitute the centre and soul of Watford. Armed with the information of *Watford Past*, I hope the visitor to Watford will come away with a very different perception.

The secret is to know where to look. Within yards of the High Street, almost opposite the concrete entrance to the Harlequin, lies an oasis of tranquillity dating in part to the 13th century. Here is a village green style churchyard, dominated by the historic St Mary's church surrounded by the former Watford Free School built in 1704, and almshouses founded in 1580 'for eight poor women' by Frances, Countess of Bedford. These allow more than a glimpse into Watford's historic past. Enter the church and you will be struck by the magnificent architecture and the stillness. Walk down the knave, enter the Essex chapel, and you will be confronted by the splendid monuments of the Morrison and Capel families intimately connected to Watford for nearly 400 years. This is the church where many of the prominent citizens of Watford over the last 700 years have come to their final resting place. One of my key aims in *Watford Past* is to give the reader some idea of what these citizens witnessed when they walked the streets and surrounding areas of the town. A stroll along the High Street and Market Place will still reveal Tudor architecture, and the frequent shadows of times gone by embedded within modern buildings.

Due to its proximity to London, Watford played host to a number of aristocratic families. The Grove, now a luxury hotel, was the seat of the Earls of Clarendon. In 1325, it is recorded as *La Grava*, being then the home of John Heydon who died in 1400 and who lies interred in St Mary's Church. The largest and most splendid house was Cassiobury, home of the Earls of Essex from the 17th century. Its parkland was mostly saved for the benefit of Watford people.

Watford took part in a number of key events of English history, and an understanding of how and where these took place will lead to an increased appreciation of Watford as it developed from being a 'genteel markate town...very long, having but one street' when Daniel Defoe visited in 1722, to a modern metropolis which, despite an unfortunate bout of development in the 1970s, still retains much of its history. Watford Museum allows a fascinating insight into Watford's past, as do the many Museum organised activities. Despite a now somewhat harsh appearance, the inner soul of Watford remains, preserved by inhabitants that take a real pride in keeping Watford as a community.

1. The earliest known map of the Watford area, by Dury and Allen, 1766.

Early times

GEOLOGY

Geologically, Watford lies in the London Basin which stretches approximately 100 miles to the west and as far as the North Downs to the south. The Berkshire Downs and Chilterns represent the northern boundaries. The substructure is made up of chalk, gravel and sand which it is believed was laid down during the Cretaceous period around 70 million years ago. The most important feature which lies to the north of Watford are the Chilterns. The local geological deposits comprise sand, clay and pebble beds which have cemented into a hard siliceous matrix known as Hertfordshire Puddingstone. Due to its hard-wearing qualities it has often been found utilised in the form of hand-mills on Roman Hertfordshire sites.

LOCATION

Watford sits in the south-west corner of Hertfordshire, 17 miles north of central London. The River Colne flows in from the north-east and passes through the lower section of the town, ultimately reaching the Thames. The River Gade cuts through Watford from the north-west, running through the two major areas of parkland, that of The Grove, former home to the Earls of Clarendon, and Cassiobury Park, the grounds of the now demolished Cassiobury House, former home to the Earls of Essex. Running parallel to the Gade is the Grand Union Canal. The Gade leaves Watford in the direction of Rickmansworth, where it merges with the Colne.

ARCHAEOLOGY

Watford has been settled since earliest times. Finds now on display in the Watford Museum prove a presence from early Palaeolithic times which covers the period up to around 8500 BC. The area at this time would have been inhabited by such exotic species as the bison, musk-ox, mammoth and woolly rhino. Early Palaeolithic finds have come from a number of localities around Watford. In Bushey, there have been finds from gravel below the River Colne.

Implements of the Clactonio-Acheulian type have been found in Croxley Green. More finds have come from two sites in the Rickmansworth area from gravel 60 and 40 feet above the Colne.

THE MESOLITHIC AND NEOLITHIC PERIODS

Commencing around 10,000 years ago it is apparent from the large number of finds in and around Watford that this was a favoured haunt of early man. The fauna of the area would have included species such as elk, wild oxen and boar. It was at this time that we find evidence of spears, arrows and fish hooks. Traces remain in the form of microliths, small flint tools used to form the tips of spears and arrows. There have been a number of Mesolithic finds in the Rickmansworth-Watford area, and in particular at Bathend Clump, Sandy Lodge Tolpits Lane and Hamper Mill. The Hamper Mill site suggests a river valley base camp. The large number of surviving flints indicate a possible Mesolithic flint industry. The Sandy Lodge site showed evidence of hearths and chipping areas where microliths were worked on.

The Neolithic period at around 6000 years ago saw forest clearance and a more settled

2. *Mesolithic hand axe from Hartspring Lane, Watford.*

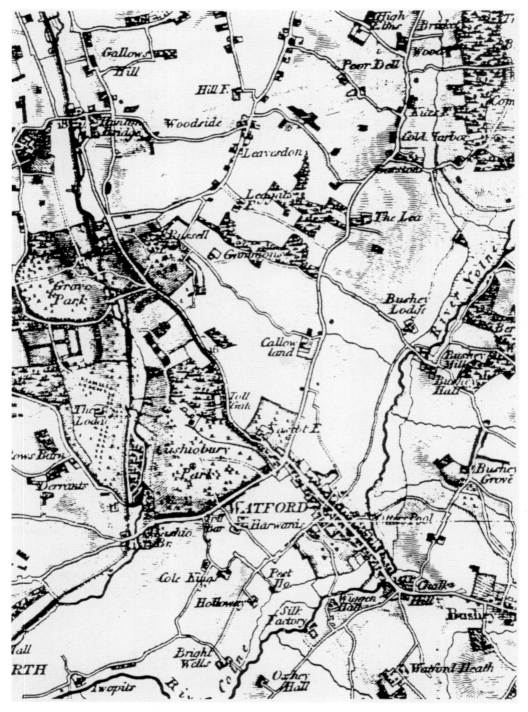

3. *The Ordnance Survey of the Watford area, 1822.*

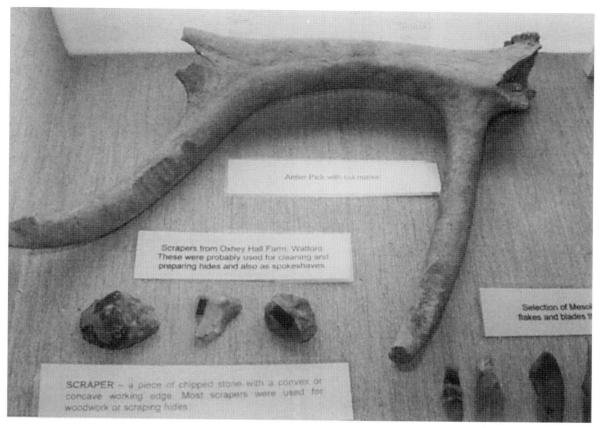

4. Mesolithic implements found in the Watford area including Oxhey Hall Farm.

lifestyle. Evidence of Neolithic settlement in the area is plentiful with sites at Tolpits Lane and Bathend Clump. These have produced worked Neolithic flints and arrowheads. Two flint hammerstones and an axe have been found at Cassiobury, whilst a polished axe was found in the Watford railway cutting.

THE BRONZE AGE

Bronze implements came into use around 4000 years ago. An extremely important hoard of Bronze Age implements was found in 1960 during the construction of a factory at Greenhill Crescent on the Holywell. It was discovered around four feet below the surface where Cassiobridge Farm used to be. The hoard is thought to date from between 1000 – 600 BC and was probably buried by a Bronze Age smith who intended to return for it. It comprised a bronze bowl, spearheads, axes, buckles, a strap toggle, wood gouges, and a knife blade. These are currently on display in the Watford Museum.

By the time we reach the Bronze Age it becomes clear from the continuity of finds that Watford was on a route frequented by prehistoric man. Its location, on the edge of Watling Street, the Icknield Way and alongside the banks of the rivers Colne and Gade, made it an attractive place to settle.

THE IRON AGE

There is comparatively little evidence of settlement during this period from around 600 BC to the time of the Roman invasion by the Emperor Claudius in 43AD. This was a period of Celtic settlement where recognisable methods of agriculture using ploughshares and oxen came into being. Wheat was the main crop. Iron

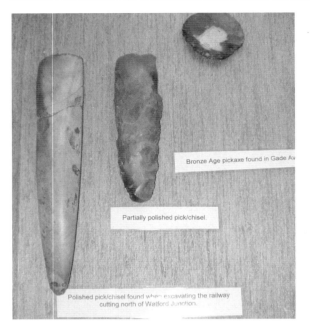

Bronze Age pickaxe found in Gade Av

Partially polished pick/chisel.

Polished pick/chisel found when excavating the railway
cutting north of Watford Junction.

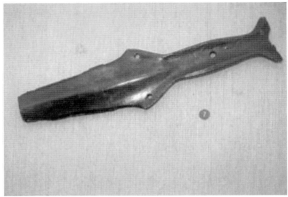

5. *(Left) Left is a Bronze Age pickaxe found while
excavating the railway cutting north of Watford Junction.
The pickaxe to the right was found in Gade Avenue.*

6. *(Below) Spearheads from the Watford Bronze Age
Hoard, now on display at the Watford Museum.*

7. *(Top right) A knife or dagger from the Watford Bronze
Age Hoard.*

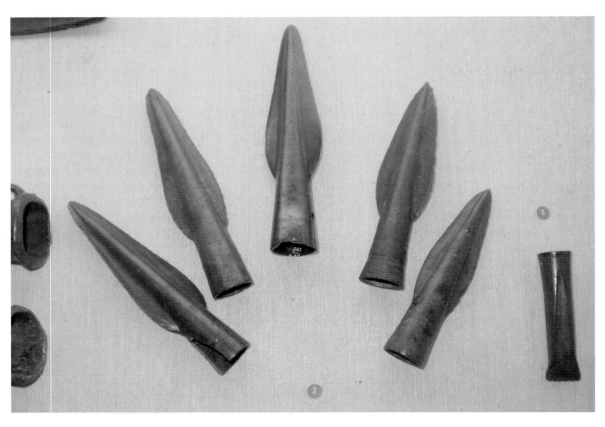

8. Bronze Age implements from the Watford Hoard.

Age pottery sherds have been found in Eastbury Road in Watford, and evidence of Iron Age occupation has been found at Sandy Lodge. Callowland, the area to the east of Watford Junction Station has yielded a Celtic coin dating to about AD40, but little more has come to light.

ROMAN WATFORD

Watford's proximity to two major Roman roads, Watling Street, and Akeman Street (the A41) which passes through both Bushey and Watford, as well as the closeness of the major Roman town of Verulamium (St Albans) suggests a presence in Roman times and a large number of finds in the surrounding area indicate an early settlement, but to date no evidence has been found within the town of Watford itself. An archaeological examination around the High Street during the building of the Harlequin shopping precinct yielded nothing earlier than the 12th century.

The surrounding area however has revealed tantalising discoveries. Evidence of a farm was found at Hamper Mill, and the remains of a Romano-British villa were discovered at Netherwylde Farm, Colney Street, near Aldenham. The site was badly damaged and little had survived. There was evidence of a mosaic floor in the form of a single tessera. In addition there were fragments of painted wall plaster which would suggest that the original owners were reasonably prosperous. Other Roman finds have come from Munden House just outside Watford, and more recently (still awaiting publication), an archaeological excavation took place at The Grove. This produced evidence of Roman burials and large numbers of everyday objects. What is clear is that the Colne was a magnet for early settlement.

9. Roman burial urn, 1st to 2nd century AD, from the Ovaltine Works site in Kings Langley.

10. A tile showing the footprints of an animal that walked over it while it was drying approximately 1800 years ago. From the Roman villa site at Netherwylde Farm. On display at the Watford Museum.

FROM THE ANGLO-SAXONS TO THE NORMANS

Very little evidence of Saxon settlement remains – a tantalising gap in Watford's history. There is however a small hoard of Saxon coins that indicates, if not a settlement, then at the very least a Saxon man passed through. In the summer of 1980, in an undisclosed area – beyond the description of the 'northwest border of Watford' – six Anglo-Saxon pennies were found and taken to the Watford Museum where they can be seen. They date from 915 to 930 AD. The periodic excavations in the town centre have failed to unearth any evidence whatsoever of Saxon settlement.

THE MANOR OF 'CASHIOBURY'

The name 'Cashio' first appears in 793 as 'Caegesho' – it has been speculated that the word means 'Caeg's spur of land'. Where used in the form of 'Cashiobury', the suffix derives from the medieval word 'burh' meaning manor.[1]

Nathaniel Salmon writing in his *History of Hertfordshire* (1728) believes that Cashiobury was the "ancient Demesne of the Saxon kings, before it was given to St Alban's..." He continues, "There is a Tradition, that this was sometimes the Residence of Offa: And then it will be no Wonder that the Hundred should be named from it upon the Conquest. It was more suitable to the Normans, that a Hundred should be distinguished by the Residence of a Mercian King, than by the Name of Albaneston, as it had been before..." Robert Clutterbuck, Watford's best known antiquarian historian says (1815) that the "Manor is supposed to have been called by this name, from having been the residence of Cassivelaunus, the chief of the Cassii, from whence the Hundred in which this domain is situated takes its name.'[2] There is no evidence for or against Clutterbuck's theory.

WATFORD'S NAME

Several derivations of the name Watford have been advanced. Sir Henry Chauncy (1632-1719) derives it from "Wet ford,"[3] the deep ford which wetted its users. Cussans (1881) suggests 'Wadeford' the ford 'midbody deep'. Other proposals are 'Wattleford', the ford protected by wattles or hurdles, and 'Watlingford' because it is on a branch of Watling Street. A document of 1479 affords the latter derivation some support, for Watling Street is definitely mentioned in it. Professor Skeat, the eminent Anglo-Saxon scholar, gives the derivation as 'Wata', a Saxon man's name and 'ford', hence 'Wata's ford', which in the passage of time became Watford. This first appears in a will dated to between 940 and 946 where the lands of 'Watforda' are left to Leofrune.

The *Victoria County History* is not in a speculative mood when it offers the evolution of the name without debate as 'Watforda' 10th and 11th century, 'Watfordia' in the 13th century, and 'Watfurth' in the 16th century.[4]

11. *The 1897 copy of the Oxhey Charter on the wall of the north aisle, St Matthew's parish church, Oxhey..*

THE OXHEY CHARTER

W R Saunders in his well researched *History of Watford* (1931) writes that,

"In the year 1871 at a sale in London of books and MSS., a parchment MS was bought, which was found to be a charter relating to Oxhey, and therefore called the 'Oxhey Charter of 1007'. In 1891 this was bought for the Bodleian Library, where it now lies ... In substance the charter is a reconveyance of an estate bestowed in (*circa*) 790, along with Cashio to St Albans Abbey by Offa..."

A copy of the charter with a translation (1897) by the Revd Newton Price is on view in the north aisle of St Matthew's parish church, Oxhey. The original charter is now in the Ashmolean Museum, Oxford, though it has to be said that there is some doubt as to its authenticity.

The next mention of Watford is in the will of Edwin of Caddington, just prior to the Norman Conquest. Edwin granted Watford, his possession, to St Albans Abbey. The Domesday Book reference of 1086 refers not to Watford, but to *Cashio*, which has led to speculation as to why Watford was not directly referred to. In all probability Cashio included the area we now regard as Watford.

12.   *The Cashio hamlet entry in the Domesday Survey of 1086.*

"The Abbot holds Cashio. It was rated for 20 hides; the abbot has 19 of them. The arable is 22 hides, in demesne 6 hides. There are three French men born and 36 villeins and 8 bordars who hold 15 ploughs. Three bordars besides and two serfs, four mills. There is meadow for 22 plough teams, common pasture sufficient for the livestock and woodland for 1,000 swine. It is worth £28: in the time of Edward the Confessor £30. Turold held one hide of Goisfride de Maneville in Cashio. Alfred, huntsman to Queen Editha, held this land."

The extent of a hide depended on the soil quality but was considered to be the amount of land that could support a peasant family for a year. Therefore it varied between 60 acres and 180 acres. A villein was a tenant farmer who held his land subject to services to the manorial lord, while a bordar was a cottager, also bound to the lord, who was one of the lowest ranks in feudal society.

The Abbot who was the Lord of the Manor mentioned at the beginning of the entry was the Abbot of St Albans, a figure who was to decrease in popularity until relieved of his possessions at the Reformation.

WATFORD'S MARKET

It was a great economic privilege to the manorial lord, in this case the Abbot of St Albans, to hold a market and fair in the vicinity. But it needed a charter, which was usually paid for.

"King Hen[ry] I, [1100-1135] granted that the Abbots and their Successors should have a Market in this Town; and King Edw[ard] IV. By Letters Patent dated at Dodington, 1 November, 1469, Edw[ard] IV[1461-1483] granted to them two Fairs to be held in this Town for Victuals, and other Things...'[5]

13. Watford Market early in the 20th century.

The market is often referred to in subsequent reports and histories. Nathaniel Salmon in his work *The History of Hertfordshire* (1728) refers to Watford as being "a Market Town", and Thomas Cos in his *Magna Britannia* (1720) says of Watford,

"'Tis a Market-Town and hath a Market weekly on Tuesday, well stored with Country Provisions and other Necessaries; and two Fairs on the Monday after Trinity Sunday, and two Days after, and on the Decllation of St John Baptist."

The *Universal British Directory* of 1792 is slightly more forthcomng:

"The market is on Tuesday, for corn, cows, sheep and hogs. There are two fairs in the year, one on the Tuesday after Trinity-Sunday, and the other on the 9th September; the lattr is called the statute, and is for hiring of servants; but on both days toys are sold, & c."

Samuel Lewis, writing in 1831, adds a small amount of further information:

"The market, granted by Henry I, is held on Tuesday; the market-house is an indifferent building supported on wooden pillars, with granaries over it, and its situation is very confiend. Fairs are held on Tuesday after Whit-Tuesday, and on August 29th and 30th, for cattle and pedlary; the latter, originally granted by Edward IV in 1469, had fallen into disuse, but was revived in 1827.

Lewis in his mention of "an indifferent" building was probably referring to a repaired version of a structure which featured in *The Times* on 1 October, 1790:

"Watford Market House – so newly repaired, – had a sad mischance last week, – the roof fell in, but as it fortunately fell *out*, no lives were lost."

Until 1928 the market continued to take place every Tuesday and Saturday in the main street but the increase in traffic forced it to a nearby site which had been cleared of slums. The last cattle market took place in 1950.

As for the fairs, Henry Williams (1884) tells us that these were abolished in 1873 "at the instance of the Local Board of Health, and very properly so, as they had degenerated into gatherings principally for drunkenness and immoral practices."

CASHIO AND WATFORD

There is some confusion as to what delineated Watford and Cashio. As already noted, the Domesday Book refers only to the manor of Cashio, with no reference at all to Watford. The St Albans Abbey Rolls state that Watford was subject to the jurisdiction of St Albans. Documents dated between 1260 and 1290 include "A list of lands, rents, and tenements belonging to the Abbot Roger in Cashio *and* Watford... 20d per annum for 3 acres in Cayso... John Deken, 3/10 annual rent for house in Watford."[6]

Chauncy at the end of the 17th century tells us that:

"... by the great Quantity of Land contained here in Caisho, it seems all the Land mentioned before in Watford is comprehended within it; since which time several Princes of the Realm have confirmed the Gift of the Mannors to the Church of St. Albans; and upon an Inquisition Anno 6 Edw. I. the Jury found that the Mannors of Caishoe, Rykemeresworth, and Saunderidge were ancient Demesne, held of the King time out of Mind before the Conquest of England, in the Hands of the Predecessors of the Abbots of St Albans, and the Abbot acknowledged it..."

John Cussans in his *History of Hertfordshire*, (1881), is of the opinion that,

"The sites of the towns of Cashio and Watford do not appear to be identical. I am inclined to believe that the British encampment of Cashio was on the brow of the gently rising acclivity from the river, about a mile southwest of Watford church. It will be seen ... that Tolpits, on the Colne, is described as being in the town of Cashio. When subsequently the country became more civilised, and travellers in increasing numbers passed over the Ford

on the road from London to and beyond Berkhampstead, Tring, and Aylesbury, the old town of Cashio gradually drifted towards the highway, and became merged in the town of Watford.'[7]

THE PEASANTS' REVOLT 1381

The Black Death of 1348-50, which was to kill an estimated 1½ million people, substantially reduced the workforce and therefore shifted the balance of power between landowners and their tenants and serfs. The shortage of labour encouraged the tenants to strike for a better bargain. Furthermore, a combination of economic grievances amongst smallholders, and a further Poll Tax on everyone over the age of 14 brought about the Peasants' Revolt of 1381.

The relationship between the landowner – the Abbot of St Albans – and the agrarian population was resented for its unfairness, for in addition to supporting themselves and their families the villeins were obliged to cultivate without payment the strips of land possessed by the Abbot. Villeins were unable to dispose of their land without the permission of the Abbot, and there were restrictions on how they could sell corn or cattle. On the death of the tenant his heirs had to pay the Abbey a heriot – usually the best beast – as a form of death duty.

Beneath the villeins the bordars were virtually serfs, unable to be free of their obligations to the lord and if they escaped were diligently sought out. Saunders also added that "Bondmen are incapable of having heirs, for all their goods belong to the house."[8]

When the Revolt began some of the fiercest supporters of the cause came from Watford where resentment against the Abbot was particularly virulent. The *Gesta* (the Abbey Records) tells us that Hertfordshire men were recognized among the rioters in London, and they also seem to have had no hesitation in offering their services to their comrades in Cambridge. The rebels vented their hatred with an attack on St Albans Abbey. Further, they were prominent in the march on London where they managed to extort a charter of manumission (freedom) from the boy king, Richard II. This they then presented to the Abbot of St Albans who reluctantly granted the charter. Whatever took place at the abbey, it would appear that the Abbot, along with the much hated John of Gaunt, once again managed to offend the rebels who launched yet another attack on the abbey.

"The hatred for the duke seems to have been as deep as the resentment against the abbot of St Albans, for much of the general distress was attributed to him, owing to his disasters in France, and the imposition of the poll taxes, which were first introduced in a Parliament packed with his supporters.' St Albans Abbey was attacked by the mob ... The prior fled; and a large body of rebels marched back from London ... they broke into the houses and closes belonging to the abbey, and became so threatening that the prison was opened to them by the abbot ... the rebels threatened to burn the manor of Kingsbury and grange of St Peter. They obtained from the abbot a charter granting common of pasture, rights of way, fishing, chase, &c., the use of handmills, and the rights of self-government without the intervention of the bailiffs of the abbey; these demands were made not only by St Albans; the men of Hertford, Watford, Berkhampstead, Redbourn, Tring, Rickmansworth... all obtained charters from the abbey....'[9]

The leaders of the uprising were Wat Tyler and John Ball, and their march into London was anything but benign. They beheaded the Treasurer Robert Hales and the Chancellor, Simon Sudbury. Wat Tyler was struck down on 15 June whilst meeting Richard II at Smithfield. John Ball was hunted down, and brought to St Albans where he was hanged, drawn and quartered. With the deaths of their leaders, just as the Abbot was forced to giveth, he did not hesitate to taketh away. Fifteen Hertfordshire men were hanged at St Albans. Barely a year later, the serfs of Watford found themselves in the same position as before the uprising. The Abbey Rolls of 1431 show that despite the events of fifty years earlier, the status quo between Abbot and tenants was truly restored.

In 1431 "the Abbot's tenants at Watford complained to Parliament of the oppressions of Wm. Flete of Rickmansworth." This resulted in a lawsuit between the Abbot and Wm. Flete. Another entry for the year 1467 tells us that "the Abbot visits Watford. The church polluted by the violence of two parish clerks [clergymen], blood has been shed; the church is purified by the Abbot."[10]

THE DEADLIER OF THE SPECIES
The case of John Chertsey in 1455 once again emphasises the dominance of the Abbot. Chertsey set up a horse mill at Watford, "and the stones were seized by the Abbot's bailiff. While they were lying in the constable's house, Mistress Chertsey collected a band of women and re-captured them. The surrender of the stones and an apology to the Abbot ended the affair."[11] The Abbot had the monopoly of mills, and would not have allowed what was in effect, a form of private enterprise that could have led to the diminution of his own income.

Relief, and even then in a limited form, would not come until the Reformation in 1539.

WATFORD PARISH REGISTERS AND VESTRY RECORDS
In 1538 Thomas Cromwell, the Vicar-General, instituted parish registers, to be written on paper and then transcribed onto parchment. The Watford registers, on parchment, have survived well although some pages have been cut out, and a number of years are missing. Of the earliest register, 1539-1557, the writing is in a single hand and pencilled on the back cover is 'John Chidbrook, vicar, 1536.' The list of Vicars for St Mary's gives the vicar at this time as John Chirdland – spelling during this period varied a great deal. The second register, 1588-1666 is also on parchment and written in the same hand as the first to the year 1618, after which it is in the hand of Cornelius Burgess, the vicar, to 1644. This suggests that periodically, the paper records which may well have been deteriorating, were transcribed in one go onto parchment. Cornelius Burgess was one of Watford's more colourful characters, who will be discussed further. The third volume, dated

1653-1702, is also on parchment and has a couple of comments marked on it. Firstly that "this Register Booke cost 15s." and "that I found this booke in the house of Samuel King, situate in Watford, where Ralph Gibbons, the registrar mentioned in this booke, lately dwelled. Witness my hand, Robert Hobson."

In addition to the registers which give us information on christenings, marriages and burials, the early vestry records provide us with some details of local government in Watford. While the manorial courts, under the auspices of the Abbot, governed the agricultural management of the area, and saw to it that tenancies were properly transferred (with, of course, a fee to the Abbot), and that law and order was maintained, the Vestry administered Church affairs and would have met originally in the vestry where the church garments were kept. Gradually the Vestry, usually a gathering of prominent residents, took over the administration of local charities, the schooling and apprenticing of orphans, the fixing of a church rate and the maintenance of the building and its churchyard. As from the seventeenth century, empowered by new Parliamentary legislation in providing for the poor and the maintenance of highways, the Vestry – in effect the parish – vied with the manor for local power and eventually the manor's powers died out. The Vestry in this form remained the governing body of Watford until the reform of local government in the later part of the nineteenth century. The Vestry elected the churchwardens and surveyors of highways, and selected the overseers of the poor, although the latter could only formally be appointed by the Justices of the Peace.'[12]

THE PLAGUE

The parish registers give the number of deaths from plague between 1540-1541 as 54. The letter 'p' is placed against the name of each of these individuals, with a note in the margin explaining its meaning. This was a high proportion of the population for at that time it could probably be numbered only in the hundreds. In 1540 between July and September 47 burials took place in St Mary's churchyard, of which it is noted in the Parish Register that 40 were due to plague. There were further outbreaks. In 1625 28 persons died and the register for 1665, the year of the Great Plague of London when one may have expected a greater number, says, "James Southey, the first who died of the Plague, whereof in all about 14 persons [died]."

Apart from the register, a more tangible result of the plague came to light in the middle of the nineteenth century when a water pipe was laid through St Mary's churchyard and exposed a number of burials, four deep, and buried without coffins. The main concern when the plague struck was to dispose of the bodies as quickly as possible and pits were dug into which the unfortunate victims were thrown with lack of ceremony.

THE REFORMATION AND WATFORD

Henry VIII's Reformation had important consequences for the structure, layout and governance of Watford. For the first time since King Offa had bestowed Cashio, or Watford on the Abbots of St Albans, in 1539 Watford was effectively under new ownership and the harsh rule of the Abbey of St Albans was over. The reality was, as ever, that the faces may have changed, but the problems were still the same. The rule of the abbot was replaced by that of the vicar and his churchwardens. Church attendance was made compulsory. The main difference was that the changes sounded the death-knell of the feudal system. For the King's friends, the Reformation and Dissolution of the Monasteries was good news. Suddenly there was an extraordinary amount of wealth in the form of chattels, estates, and land looking for new homes. For example, Sir Richard Morrison, a favourite of Henry, was able to buy Cassiobury for the sum of £176 17s. 6d. "King H[enry] VIII. Who by Letters Patents dated the 20th of *Aug.* in the 37th Year of his Reign, conveyed to *Richard Morisin*, Esq. this Mannor of Caishoebury.' Of Richard Morrison's rise to fortune we are told by Chauncy:

"...the time of his [Morrison's] Youth, bred up in the University, where he studied Philosophy; and when he had attained to some Perfection of Knowledge in the Latin and Greek

Tongues, and the liberal Arts, he removed thence to the Inns of Court, where he became well skilled in the Common and Civil Law, and by Reason of his great Learning, obtained much Esteem and Favour with King H[enry] VIII and Edw[ard] VI so that they often employed him upon several Ambassages to the Emperor Charles V ... he began a fair and large House in this Place, situated upon a dry Hill not far from a pleasant River in a fair Park; and had prepared Materials for the finishing hereof, but before the same could be half built, he was forced to fly beyond the Seas, and returning out of Italy died at Strasburgh, on the 17th Day of *March, anno* 1556, 2d and 3d of *Philip* and *Mary,* to the great Grief of all good Men: After his Decease this Mannor came to the Possession of *Bridget* his Widow, who enjoyed it..."

1   Bell, Alan William, and Watford Council: *Street and Place Names in Watford,* p29 (1973)

2   Clutterbuck, Robert: *The History and Antiquities of the County of Hertford,* (1815).

3   Chauncy, Sir Henry: *The Historical Antiquities of Hertfordshire etc,* Vol. 2 p348 (1700)

4   *Victoria County History,* Hertfordshire Vol. 2 p446

5   *Ibid,* p.348

6   Saunders, William R: *History of Watford,* p9 (1931) (rept 1970)

7   Cussans, John Edwin: *History of Hertfordshire,* p166 (1881).

8   Saunders *op cit*

9   *Victoria County History,* Hertfordshire, Vol. 2 pp 14-15

10   Saunders *op cit*, extracts from the Abbey Rolls

11   Saunders *op cit* quoting from Abbey Rolls

12   Trevor May, University of Hertfordshire, from an introduction to the 1849 General Board of Health Report for Watford.

Cassiobury House and Park

The two premier Watford families, the Earls of Essex, and the Earls of Clarendon have since the 1920s and 1930s left Watford, but their ancestral ghosts linger in Watford's infrastructure. The Earls of Essex became a north of England family but numerous street names bear witness to their local connections.

Cassiobury House was built and rebuilt a number of times before total demolition in 1927. Because of the prominence of the Essex family, there are a number of high profile accounts and illustrations which give us an idea of the various stages of its development. Note that the spelling of Cassiobury varies enormously, particularly in documents of the 17th and 18th centuries. The most common reference thereafter is to Cashiobury, before finally settling into Cassiobury.

Richard Morrison, a diplomat for Henry VIII was knighted in 1556, and is credited with having initiated the building of the house. It was Sir Charles Morrison, his son, who completed the building. He died in 1599 at which time the house passed to his daughter Elizabeth, who married Arthur, Lord Capel of Hadham in Essex. It was this marriage of a Morrison to a Capel that was to bring the house and substantial parts of Watford into the ownership of the Earls of Essex until 1922.

John Evelyn visited the 'house of Cassioberie' at the invitation of the 1st Earl of Essex in April 1680.

'I went with the Earl of Essex to his house at Cassiobury in Hertfordshire... The house is new, a plaine fabric, built by my friend, Mr. Hugh May. There are divers fair and good rooms, and excellent carving by Gibbons... There is in the porch, or entrance, a painting by Verrio, of Apollo and the Liberal Arts... Some of the chimney mantels are of Irish marble, brought by my Lord from Ireland, when he was Lord Lieutenant, and not much inferior to Italian... The tympanum, or gable at the front, is a bass-relievo of Diana hunting,

cut in Portland stone... The library is large, and very nobly furnished, and all the books are richly bound and gilded... No man has been more industrious than this noble Lord in planting about his seat, adorned with walks, ponds, and other rural elegancies...'[1]

Evelyn was not without criticism. Almost in direct contrast to the imagery of Restoration grandeur, he tells us that it is of "plaine fabric" and being rebuilt "just where the old one was", for he also comments on the unfortunate position of the house: it is "a pitty the house was not situated to more advantage", for "the soil is stonie, churlish and uneven, nor is the water neere enough to the house, though a very swift & cleare streame run[s]... in the vally." He is referring to the Gade, which then produced "faire troutes".[2]

A 17th-century description of the house, by Henry Chauncy, portrays it as "a faire and large house in this place upon a dry hill, not far from a pleasant river in a faire park." However, Sir Richard Morrison was not to enjoy his new domain for very long. Henry VIII's eldest daughter Mary, a devout Catholic, ascended the throne in 1553 and in 1555 persecution of Protestants began. Many of those who refused to adhere to the Catholic form of worship were burnt to death as heretics. Sir Richard died at Strasburg in 1556 having fled the persecution.

Nathaniel Salmon's description, written around 1728, describes Cassiobury House favourably:

"The Seat is elegant, the Situation as well chosen as the County affords; upon a dry Spot within a Park, facing the South East Sun, with the River at a proper Distance below it, and a pleasant Hill behind it ... Sir Charles Moryson, Son and Heir, succeeded, and completed the Building." He continues, "Sir Charles died 1599. Upon his Death his Lady enjoyed this Place for Life. After her, Sir Charles Moryson her Son, made a Baronet 1611, and a Knight of the Bath at the Coronation of King Charles I."

Baron Capel initially supported the Puritan cause in the English Civil War, but changed

14. *Probably the best-known view of Cassiobury, by J M W Turner c.1806-7, from John Britton's* History and Description of Cassiobury Park, *1837.*

15. A view of Cassiobury Park by John Wootton, c.1748, a painting now on view at the Watford Museum.

over to an all-embracing support for Charles I. He met the same fate as the King, only a short time after Charles's execution.

Upon the Restoration Capel's son, also Arthur (1631-83), was made 1st Earl of Essex, a title that was once again re-created. (An earlier Earl of Essex, unconnected with the Capel family, was Queen Elizabeth's favourite.)

When the new Earl began to use Cassiobury as his principal residence he decided, with the exception of the north wing, to build a new house. The gardens were laid out in the manner of Versailles by the noted gardener Moses Cook who, we are told, published a book called *Forest Trees* in 1675.

The 1st Earl pursued a successful political career until in June 1683 he was accused by a fellow peer of being involved in the Rye House Plot, which sought the murder of the King and his brother, the Catholic Duke of York. He was apprehended whilst quietly enjoying the pleasures of domestic life at Cassiobury, whence he

was escorted by a party of horse, and committed as a close prisoner to the Tower. He was discovered, on the 13th of July, in a closet in his lodgings, with his throat cut, possibly by suicide. His body was interred in the family vault in Watford church.

Much of John Britton's volume on Cassiobury (1837) (dedicated to the 5th Earl of Essex) is taken up with the grounds. He says that in 1715, the gardens were eulogised by Stephen Switzer, in his interestingly titled volume called

The Nobleman, Gentleman, and Gardener's Recreation; or, an Introduction to Gardening, Planting, Agriculture, and the other Business and Pleasures of a Country Life. Switzer urges,

"...it must not be pass'd by, that Cashiobury was one of the first places in England when the polite Spirit of Gardening shone the Brightest; for altho' there have been great Additions made there within a few Years last past, the main Foundation was laid by that Worthy and

16.   Arthur Capel, 1st Earl of Essex (1631-83). He was arrested in 1683 for his alleged involvement in the Rye House Plot, and allegedly committed suicide that year in the Tower.

Honorable Patriot of his Country, under the more immediate conduct of Mr. Cook, his Gardener, yet living; who has likewise oblig'd the World with a Discourse concerning the raising of Forest Trees, &c. which is still extant. I must confess I never see that truly delightful Place without being more than ordinarily ravish'd with its Natural Beauty."

Cassiobury throughout its 400-year existence was a byword for style, elegance and culture, and throughout the period when it was the country seat of the Earls of Essex it was visited by most of England's royalty and aristocracy.

Britton tells us that "Cassiobury is situated within the hundred and manor of Cassio, and county of Hertford, at a distance of sixteen miles north of London, and one mile from the town of Watford." In the *Baronetage* of 1720, he tells us, "the house built by the Morrisons is briefly described as having been 'a stately structure, in the midst of a park, with beautiful gardens and wood-walks'."

The painting of Cassiobury House shown on the jacket of this book and in illustration 15 is

17.   South front of Cassiobury House. From a watercolour by Hugh May, 1800.

18. The Great Library of Cassiobury House during the latter part of the 19th century.

on display in the entrance of Watford Museum and depicts the 3rd Earl of Essex, his family, friends and servants in the foreground.

The park today is devoid of any original structures but retains a beauty normally associated with the heart of the countryside. A description from the 1870s when the house still stood is recognisable: the avenue of trees, replaced since the original 17th-century trees, still stands and the lock, the canal, and the landscape around the rivers remain largely unspoiled.

"A beautiful cascade by the side of the mill pours its pellucid water into the trout stream below, and adjoining are the bridge over the canal, the locks and lock cottage, forming, together with a number of large beech and other trees growing near, a piece of rich scenery that has on many occasions attracted the notice of artists visiting Watford. In the Second Park [this is the area where the canal lies] the ground rises from the canal to a considerable height, and this slope is adorned with some fine timber, and from it is obtained a magnificent view of the fine old mansion and the Home Park, with its diversity of trees and shrubs, its splendid herd of deer, and numerous cattle...."[3]

The river's excellent fishing was strictly reserved for the Earl's family and friends. But the public were, even before the sale of the house and park, allowed access to the grounds.

"His lordship also grants keys of the gates to the neighbouring gentry, giving them the privilege of riding or driving through the park and wood... During the summer months several parties of workmen and school children

19. *The Great Cloister at Cassiobury House. Aquatint by J Hill after J M W Turner.*

20. *The Swiss Cottage at Cassiobury, 1837. The cottage was by the Gade and was a popular picnic spot. It was destroyed by fire during the Second World War.*

21. The Old Mill at Cassiobury, from a photograph taken in February 1893.

22. Cassiobury House in 1906.

23. *The Inner Library at Cassiobury, photograph of c.1900.*

24. *The main gateway to Cassiobury House, c.1906. The gate was demolished in 1970 to allow the widening of Rickmansworth Road.*

25. *Cassiobury Park in 1905.*

26 *The footbridge in Cassiobury Park in 1934.*

from London come here for a day's excursion, and generally leave greatly impressed with the beauty and salubrity of the park and neighbourhood, and grateful to his lordship for the liberty granted to them.'[4]

A 19th-century description of the interior of the house concentrates on the curiosities contained within, including David Garrick's chair, a lock of hair that belonged to Charles I, a piece of velvet from his coffin, a piece of ribbon of the Order of the Garter worn at his execution and a fragment of the pall used at his funeral. In addition to this morbid collection was included a handkerchief stained with the blood of William III when he was wounded at the Battle of the Boyne, a lock of Napoleon's hair, and a piece of the willow that hung over his tomb at St Helena.

The house was again altered in 1801-2.

THE END OF CASSIOBURY HOUSE

Country houses were expensive to run, and there were rumours that the 7th Earl was in financial difficulties a number of years prior to the First World War – probably from gambling debts. By the beginning of the war, the Earl and his family were living in their central London home, and Cassiobury was to let. This coincided with an increasing demand for building land as Watford continued to expand as a dormitory town. George V and Queen Mary were thought to be interested in purchasing the mansion, but it was not to be. In June 1922 Adele, Countess Dowager of Essex and her son, the 8th Earl, sold the estate of 870 acres of land for £65,500. The House was then stripped of its contents and left derelict. By 1927, no buyer had been found for the house itself and it was wantonly demolished, and the materials sold off for building purposes. The Park still survives, providing a recreational lung for the town, and a housing development in the area of the tennis courts sits on the site of the house.

The 10th Earl, at one time a footballer for a Hampshire county team, a Socialist, and a greengrocer in Morecambe, lived modestly in

27. *From* The Times, *18 October 1921, announcing that the Countess of Essex had decided to sell Cassiobury Park.*

A FAMOUS OLD MANSION.

The Countess of Essex has decided to sell the Cassiobury Park Estate at Watford. The above photograph shows the fine old red brick mansion, built in 1667.

28. The sale of building materials from the demolished Cassiobury House in 1927.

the north of England, having inherited virtually nothing. He died in June 2005 and was succeeded as 11th Earl by his son Paul Capell, a schoolteacher. After his death the title will pass to a distant cousin in California.[5]

ECHOES OF CASSIOBURY
The main gatehouse *(ill. 24)*, an early 19th-century structure, survived on the Rickmansworth Road until 1970 when it was demolished to make way for a road widening scheme. Henry Williams, writing around 1880, described the Gatehouse thus:

"The principal entrance, which is a short distance from the top of the High Street, is extremely pretty; there is a lodge on either side, one square and the other octagonal in shape; both have towers; they are castellated, and the front of the square one is covered with ivy."

There are still standing a number of associated buildings. Most of these are lodges and subsidiary houses used by the Essex family and their friends.

John Britton in 1837 tells us that:

"In different parts of the park and grounds are various cottages and lodges, which are distinguished at once for their exterior picturesque features and for the domestic comfort they afford to their humble occupants. Unlike the ragged, wretched sheds and hovels which are too often seen by the road-side, and even in connexion with some of the large and ancient parks of our island, the buildings here delineated are calculated to shelter, to console, and gratify the labourer after his salty toil, and to make his wife and family clearly and diligent.... The cottages at Cassiobury have been designed with the two-fold object of being both useful and ornamental. They are occupied, exempt from rent and taxes, by men and women who are employed by the noble landlord in various offices about the park, the gardens, and the house; thus the park-keeper, a game-keeper, a shepherd, a lodge-keeper, a gardener, a carpenter, a miller, a lock-keeper, &c. are accommodated."

The names of the cottages given in 1837 by Britton are Park-keeper's Cottage, Thorn Cottage, Shepherd's or Keeper's Lodge, Entrance Lodge, Ridge Lane Lodge, Great Beech Tree Cottage, Russell Farm Lodge, Russell Cottage and Cassio-bridge Cottage.

The search for the remaining buildings of Cassiobury leads to some unlikely places and detective work is required to piece things together on the estate. The Friends of Cassiobury now provide an excellent map with an overlay diagram of Cassiobury Park which shows where the house and features once lay.

Probably due to their size and ability to integrate usefully into the local landscape, a number of the former Cassiobury lodges remain. These include Cassio Bridge Lodge at 67 Gade Avenue, an early 19th-century timbered lodge, originally built for two families. In front of this was Cassiobridge Common, on which gypsy encampments stayed at times. Russell's in Greenbank Road, is a former Cassiobury red

29. Cassio Bridge Lodge , now 67 Gade Avenue.

31. Russell's in Greenbank Road, a former Cassiobury villa dating from the 18th century.

brick villa from the late 18th century, but altered in the 19th century. The north service wing has a small cupola bellcote with a vane dated 1718, possibly that removed from the summer house of Watford House demolished in 1904.

Little Cassiobury, once part of the Cassiobury estate, housed members of the Capel family. Listed residents include Sir Bladen Capel, a naval officer who in 1807 commanded a frigate called *Endymion*.

The Gateway and attached walls dating from the mid- to late-16th century remain. Alterations took place *c*.1830. These were formerly

30. Little Cassiobury, a dower house to Cassiobury, built in the late 17th century and today hidden away in the car park of West Herts College in Hempstead Road. Photo 2005.

32. The former stable block to Little Cassiobury, much altered in 1930. Photo 2005.

34. The former gateway to Cassiobury Park.

33. The Cassiobury Park bandstand, now reconstructed outside Watford Town Hall.

part of the gardens of Cassiobury Park and now stand approximately 30 metres north-west of 42 The Gardens. They have been given a Grade II listing.

Nearer the centre of town, outside the town hall, stands Cassiobury's old bandstand.

1   John Evelyn, *Diary*, quoted in Cussans, *History of Hertfordshire* (1881)
2   Tomkins, Malcolm, and Javes, Graham, *So That Was Hertfordshire: Travellers' Jottings 1322-1887* (1998)
3   Williams, Henry, *History of Watford* (1884) p17
4   *Ibid*
5   Bunyan, Nigel and Fenton, Ben, 'New Earl is ever so humble' in *Daily Telegraph* 18 June 2005.

The Grove and Watford Place

THE GROVE

The Grove sits at the end of the Hempstead Road, almost adjoining the M25 roundabout. Although on the extreme perimeter of what purists would define as Watford, the Earls of Clarendon played an important role in the civic affairs of the town – Watford's first mayor was a Clarendon. As with Cassiobury, The Grove was visited by a number of important personages including Edward VII and Winston Churchill.

The name possibly originated 1294-5 when the land was owned by a John de Brittewell, but an alternative suggestion is that it began with John atte Grove mentioned in 1353.[1] During the 14th century, the land of 'La Grava' belonged "in the vill of Cassio" to Thomas de Harpesfield and his wife Joan. The parish church of St Mary has an inscription to John

Heydon of the Grove who died in 1400. John Rayner and his wife Joan conveyed the manor in 1481-2 to John Fortescue, John Sturgeon, John Forster, and Henry Heydon, to the use of John Fortescue. By 1487 the estate was in the hands of the family of John Melksham. In 1503, his widow and son conveyed it to a Reginald Pegge for an annual rent of £10. From Pegge the manor was sold to William and John Heydon, almost certainly descendants of the John Heydon mentioned above. The manor remained in the hands of the Heydons until 1602 when it was sold to Clement Scudamore. He sold it in 1631 along with two water mills to Sir William Ashton whose family held it until 1703 when it was owned by the Buck family. Later owners included Fulk Greville, the third Lord Doneraile, Charles Unwin and in 1753, the Hon. Thomas Villiers who in 1776 became Earl of Clarendon.[2]

John Edwin Cussans, writing during the latter part of the 19th century, describes the house as a

"substantial edifice of red brick, in plan resembling the letter 'T' laid sideways, the base

35.   The Grove, home of the Earls of Clarendon until 1936.

36. A photograph of Edward VII on a visit to the Clarendons at The Grove.

of the letter towards the east... it is probable that the house, as we now see it, was built by the first Earl of Clarendon about the year 1760, though the style of the brickwork appears to indicate the early part of the reign of George the Second. It is evident that great alterations were effected about the year 1780, and that the present third story was then added ...a curious combination of fact and fiction points to Lord Doneraile as the builder of the Grove, between the years 1743 and 1749. The fact is, that when the late Earl was making alterations in the basement rooms, he discovered in the kitchen walls, strong indications of its having formerly been a chapel..."

However, Alan Ball in his book on Watford

The Grove

In these days, when private estate after private estate round London is being swiftly absorbed by building or public ownership, it is difficult amid the general loss to indulge in particular grief for one property. But LORD CLARENDON's house, The Grove, the sale of which is now announced, deserves at least "the passing "tribute of a sigh." Not that its architecture particularly distinguishes it from the many Eighteenth-Century houses which England still possesses, nor that its grounds—gorgeous as they are, with a small river flowing through them—could not be matched by others elsewhere in England. The principal interest is derived from its having been one of the great political houses of the Nineteenth Century. In these degenerate days it may be necessary to call it The Grove, Watford (as though it were first cousin to "The "Laurels" or "The Acacias"), but to our grandfathers, Broadlands, Brocket, Woburn, or The Grove needed no suffixes. In those houses almost exclusively Whig society met, Whig Cabinets were formed, and Whig policy was formulated. The host at The Grove during its most splendid years was the fourth EARL of CLARENDON, one of the most disinterested and patriotic statesmen that England has known.

Thanks to its nearness to London, The Grove must have been one of the first houses where the practice of Saturday to Monday visiting (as the week-end habit was then called) was in force. That great diarist GREVILLE records staying there with the PALMERSTONS, LADY HOLLAND, MACAULAY, LUTTRELL, and BULWER LYTTON. The amusements of such a company, which principally consisted in conversation or in visiting the Library and seeing the portraits collected by the Restoration statesmen, might make no great appeal to the modern mind. Yet there may be some who would gladly turn off the wireless, lock up the cocktails, and clear out the bridge tables, if only they might listen to MACAULAY's talk and hear examples of LADY HOLLAND's wit. GREVILLE—never the most generous of critics—wrote:—

It is always refreshing, in the midst of the cold hearts and indifferent tempers one sees in the world, to behold such a spectacle of intimate union and warm affection as the Grove presents. . . . I have always thought Clarendon the least selfish, most generous, and amiable man with whom I am acquainted.

37. The Times of 20 February 1936, announcing the sale of The Grove.

38. Watford Place at 27 King Street, built c. 1797. It underwent alterations in 1822. Photo 2005.

1922-1972, relates that the house was built by Sir Robert Taylor in 1756, enlarged by Matthew Brettingham in 1780 and had further extensive alterations in 1850.

The Earls of Clarendon remained the owners of the Grove until the 1936. *The Times* editorial of 20 February 1936 greeted the demise of The Grove as a family house with relief that the property would not be developed "for speculative purposes". The Grove and its grounds have now been turned into a hotel, golf course, conference centre, and a number of restaurants. Although the main house still stands, a large number of modern buildings have been added.

WATFORD PLACE

Very much in the manner of Cassiobury House, Watford Place tends to appear, disappear and then re-invent itself during the course of Watford's history. Chauncy, writing at the end of the 17th century mentions it:

"Michael Heydon Esq. granted to Dame *Dorothy Morison*, the Widow of Sir *Charles Morison* the elder of Caishobury in the Parish of Watford, by Deed dated 18th Oct. Anno 11 Jac. prim. [1613-14] a Lease of one capital Messuage in Watford called Watford-place, with all Barns, Stables, Rooms, Gardens, Orchards and Appurtenances to the same belonging, for one hundred years, under a yearly Rent; and the Lady placed *Thomas Valentine*, MA Preacher of God's Word and four poor Widow Women, or Alms Women in the several Rooms, Parcel of the said Messuage, to continue, during their Lives and good Behaviour, and intended that after their Departures thence, other like learned Preachers and poor Widows should be placed in their Steads during the lease..."[3]

The original Watford Place had been the home of Elizabeth Fuller the founder of the Free School, which stood in the grounds of the house.

The building now standing at 27 King Street was built *c.* 1797 and underwent alterations in 1822. This is the third house on the site and stood then in substantial grounds. Jonathan King sold the house in 1851 and the estate was broken up into building plots and King Street developed on the line of the old carriage drive to the house.

1   Ball, Alan, *Street and Place Names in Watford* p40 (1973)

2   *Victoria County History*, Hertfordshire, Vol. 2 p462

3   Chauncy p363

The Civil Wars and after

Watford sided with Parliament during the Civil Wars, probably in response to the levy of ship money in 1642 – at £62, a large sum for a relatively small town. The Vicar, Cornelius Burgess, was a Parliamentarian who used the pulpit to spread his political beliefs.

In 1643 Charles I's troops confronted the soldiers stationed in Watford which were under the command of Parliamentary general Robert Devereux, 3rd Earl of Essex (1591-1646). (It should be noted, to avoid confusion, that when Devereux died in 1646 the title became extinct and was recreated in 1661 when Arthur Capel jnr was made 1st Earl of Essex, but there was no family connection between Devereux and Capel.)

The Calendar of State papers indicate a number of comings and goings between 1644 and 1645. The Parliamentary General, the Earl of Manchester, passed through Watford in 1644 on his way to Reading. In 1645 there is a reference to 1000 Parliamentary men to be sent to Watford and again in 1645 when the Committee of Both Kingdoms decided "To write to Major-General Browne to cause 500 horse at Colnbrook to march to Watford." These were to be put at the disposal of Sir Thomas Fairfax. Oliver Cromwell is believed to have spent a night in Watford en-route to St Albans at a now-demolished house in Church Street.

Watford's main connection with the Wars was through Lord Capel, Baron Hadham, whose home was at Cassiobury. As we have seen *(p20)*, he had married the daughter of Sir Charles Morrison, whose tomb sculptured by Nicholas Stone can be seen in the Essex Chapel in St Mary's Church. Capel received his title, Lord Capel of Hadham, in August 1641 from Charles I and was one of the King's most loyal supporters.

After Capel's capture by the Parliamentary forces he was tried at Westminster Hall for treason, and was sentenced to be hung, drawn

39. Entrance to Hadham Hall, home of the Capel family prior to the move to Cassiobury House.

and quartered, but as a concession to leniency and his being a member of the nobility, his sentence was 'reduced' to beheading. Arthur Capel's last moments were recorded by Dr Morley, Bishop of Winchester, in a letter to Edward Symonds, Capel's one-time chaplain.

"I was there at the time assigned... But he was to have an agony before his passion; and that was the parting with his wife, eldest son, son-in-law, two of his uncles, and Sir Thomas Corbet, especially the parting with his most dear lady; which was the saddest spectacle that I ever beheld... in blessing the young lord, he commanded him never to revenge his death, though it should be in his power. The like he said unto his Lady... After this, with much adoe I persuaded his wife and the rest to be gone: and then being all alone with me, he said, 'Doctor, the hardest part of my work in this world, is now past...'"

After prayers "they were all carried to Sir Robert Cotton's house, where I was with him, till he was called unto the scaffold, and would have gone up with him, but the guard of soldiers would not suffer me."

40. *The Capel family in a portrait by Cornelius Johnson c.1640. From left to right: Arthur Capel (1631-83, later to be the 1st Earl of Essex), Charles Capel, Arthur Capel (?1610-49) (Lord Capel of Hadham), Elizabeth Capel (née Morrison), Henry Capel, Mary Capel and Elizabeth Capel.*

On the scaffold in Westminster Hall, as was the tradition, Capel made an impassioned speech to the assembled crowd proclaiming that it was a duty and privilege to die for his sovereign. He then prayed.

Then the grim courtesies of the scaffold began. While he was speaking, the executioner had slipped away, and when he turned from the crowd in Palace Yard to prepare for the block, Capel looked in vain for him among the group of men, including his chaplain and Colonel Beecher, the commander of the guard, standing upon the platform. "Which is the gentleman?" he asked, taking off his doublet and waistcoat. Then, when the executioner had returned and knelt to ask forgiveness, he replied, "I forgive thee from my soul"; and accompanied his words by a gift of five pounds. One boon he asked: the time for a short prayer after he had lain down upon the block. Capel then asked the executioner: "Stay a little; which side do you stand upon? I think I should lay my hands that way [pointing fore-right]": and answer being made "Yes", he stood still a little while, and then said (speaking to his servants): "Pray at the moment of striking joyn your Prayers: but make no noise; it is inconvenient at this time." His servant suggested he put on his cap. Capel replied: "Should I?" Capel to the executioner: "Well, you are ready when I am ready, are you not?"

Capel then knelt and placed his head on the block: "Am I well now?" The executioner replied: "Yes." Capel: "Here lie both my hands out. When I lift up my hand thus then you may strike." Capel then raised his two hands behind his back, the signal to the executioner to strike and his head is removed with a single blow of the axe.[1]

A slightly different version of events has Capel asking the executioner, "Did you cut off my master's [Charles I] head?" The executioner replied "Yes". Capel asked "Where is the instrument which did it?" The axe is brought and Capel asks the executioner if he is certain it is the same axe to which the executioner answers he is sure that it is. Capel then took and kissed the axe.[2]

The body was removed first to the family seat

41. *The burial vault of Arthur Capel and his wife Elizabeth Morrison in St Cecelia's church, Little Hadham. The inscription relates that Capel died on 9th March 1648, but this was made before the beginning of each year was changed to January 1st. Under modern dating, he died in March 1649.*

at Hadham Hall, and placed in the family vault at Little Hadham Church.

Hadham Hall remained the property of the Earls of Essex until sold in 1900 by the 8th Earl.[3] Capel had requested of Dr Morley that his heart be placed in a silver box until the hoped for restoration of Charles II and presented to the new king with a request for it to be buried at the feet of Charles I, his late master. This didn't happen. The box remained at Hadham Hall and was accidentally discovered in 1703 by Dr Stanley, chaplain to the then Earl of Essex, who was requested by the family to place it in the family vault. The heart was removed from the silver box and placed in an iron box prior to interment to prevent the theft of a valuable item when the vault should again be opened at some time in the future. Henry

Williams in his 1883 *History of Watford* says that in the inner library at Cassiobury House "is the casket containing the heart of the first Lord Capel, and on the wall is a brass plate giving particulars of the same ... the inscription states that the heart was removed from the vault at Hadham by George, fifth earl of Essex, in 1809, and placed in this wall."

THE 4TH AND 5TH EARLS

Thomas Gainsborough painted the 4th Earl of Essex presenting a silver cup to Thomas Clutterbuck *(ill. 43),* a member of a prominent local family and also sheriff of Hertfordshire *(see ill. 43).* In a letter to Clutterbuck that accompanied the cup, the Earl of Essex expressed his gratitude and regard for his friend:

> "It has long been my inclination to give you a small token of the regard I have for you, and hope this Cup which I desire y[ou]r acceptance of, will be agre[e]able to you, & that you will consider it as a small token, or proof how much I think myself indebted to you, & of an esteem which I shall always retain."

In 1784 the Earl of Essex commissioned the painting by Gainsborough to commemorate the presentation of the cup, which had actually taken place twelve years earlier. He then gave the painting to Clutterbuck. The two families maintained close ties throughout the nineteenth century, and the silver cup is still in the Clutterbuck family's possession. The painting remained with the family until the Getty Museum purchased it in 1972. The Clutterbucks played a leading role during the 18th and 19th centuries in the governance of Watford. Robert Clutterbuck, the historian, was a son of Thomas Clutterbuck.

THE ACTRESS AND THE EARL

At a time when acting, the term 'actress' and the area of Covent Garden were all understood to lack respectability it is odd that the marriage of the 5th Earl of Essex at the age of 82 to a 44-year-old opera singer and actress, Catherine 'Kitty' Stephens (1794-1882), didn't cause more public comment. Kitty had gained early fame, in 1813, for her performance as Mandane in

42. Kitty Stephens in 1813.

Artaxerxes at Covent Garden. The wedding took place in the April of 1838, followed by the Earl's perhaps almost inevitable death in the following April. The *Times,* which had commented on the wedding announcement, "The Honeymoon! Cupid is really a sad wag", published on 2 May that year a more restrained and proper announcement on the death and funeral of the Earl.

"FUNERAL OF THE EARL OF ESSEX. —The funeral of the above lamented nobleman took place on Tuesday at Watford. In accordance with the wish expressed by the noble Earl, it was conducted in a very private manner, and there was very little pomp or ostentation in the ceremony. The remains were removed from the mansion in Belgrave-square about 10 o'clock, and placed in a hearse drawn by six horses. The hearse was covered with a pall, on which the arms of the noble Earl were richly emblazoned. The hearse was followed by three mourning coaches and four, in the first of which was the present Earl, as chief-mourner, and in the second was Admiral Capel and some other members of the family... The mourning-coaches were followed by the carriages of several of the nobility. Early in the morning the

43.   *The 4th Earl of Essex, left, presenting a silver cup to Thomas Clutterbuck of Watford, by Thomas Gainsborough (1784)*
(reproduced by kind permission of the J. Paul Getty Museum, Los Angeles)

solemn tolling of the bell of the church gave the inhabitants of Watford notice of the melancholy event that was about to take place. The inhabitants, with very few exceptions, keep their shops closed during the day, and although it was the day on which the weekly market is held, very little business was done, and all classes appeared anxious to pay a tribute of respect to the worth of the deceased nobleman. The funeral cavalcade arrived at Watford about 1 o'clock, and the mourners were then joined by the Hon. and Rev. Mr. Capel, the vicar, all of whom were dressed in deep mourning. The church, [St. Mary's] which was hung throughout with black cloth, was crowded with inhabitants of Watford and the vicinity. About 2 o'clock, the necessary arrangements having been completed, the coffin was removed from the hearse and conveyed by eight men into the chancel of the church. The coffin was covered with splendid crimson velvet and silver nails. The coronet of the deceased nobleman was carried before it. The burial service was then performed in the most impressive manner by the Rev. Mr. Clutterbuck. The mournful ceremonies having been completed, the coffin was placed in the family vault, and the crowd retired from the church."

Catherine Stephen's memorial in the Essex Chapel of St Mary's church tells us that she "died at 9 Belgrave Square, on the 22nd February 1882 aged 91 years". She was buried in Kensal Green cemetery.

The 5th Earl had been a major patron of the arts and it was during his time that Cassiobury reached its peak. On acceding to the title he employed the architect James Wyatt to redesign Cassiobury House, incorporating Hugh May's earlier structure, and hired Humphry Repton to further develop the grounds.

After a close family connection with Watford in excess of 400 years, the present Earl is firmly ensconced in the north of England *(see p.30)*.

A ROYAL VISIT – WAS SHE AMUSED?

The historian, Henry Williams, was an eye-witness to Queen Victoria's visit to Watford, en route to the Marquis of Salisbury at Hatfield House. The event was reported in the *The Times*,

44. *George Capel Coningsby, 5th Earl of Essex (1757-1839).*

HER MAJESTY'S VISITS TO CASHIO-
BURY AND HATFIELD-HOUSE,

(FROM OUR OWN REPORTER.)

HATFIELD, Oct. 21.

It has already been announced that Her Majesty and Prince Albert will leave Cashiobury-park, near Watford, where they are at present staying with the Queen Dowager, to-morrow (Thursday), for the purpose of proceeding to Hatfield-house, the seat of the Marquis of Salisbury. The visit to the Queen Dowager is a private one; but that to the noble Marquis will partake more of that public character which has hitherto belonged to Her Majesty's visits to those of her nobility whom she has honoured with her presence.

As may well be supposed, this town and its neighbourhood are in no little excitement at the prospect of this visit from Royalty. At the mansion itself, workmen and artists have for a long time past been engaged in perfecting the decorations, which are on a scale of very great splendour and magnificence; and more recently, since it was made known to the noble Marquis of Salisbury that Her Majesty would pay her long deferred visit, all the arrangements have been accelerated, and special preparations made for the accommodation of the Royal visitors. The Marquis has been here for some days, superintending these preparations. Since the lamentable fire which occurred at Hatfield-house some years since, it has been but seldom open to the view of strangers; but there is every reason to suppose that after Her Majesty has left, it will be made more accessible to the public, in the same way

45. *Extract from The Times report on the visit of Queen Victoria to Watford in October 1846.*

of 22 October 1846 *(ill. 45),* but Williams adds colour to the description in *The Times* when he describes how Watford prepared for the visit:

"The (Royal) journey was made by road, and the horses attached to the Royal carriages were changed at the Rose and Crown Hotel, when the inhabitants took the opportunity offered by the first visit of Her Majesty to Watford to show their loyalty to her person and throne by a grand demonstration and general holiday. An arch of evergreens and flowers was erected across the street from the house of Mr. Wise, grocer, to the Market House, and another across the street from Mrs. Iles' house to Butcher's Yard; at the top of the latter a brass band was stationed, that played the National Anthem on the approach of the Royal cortège, and other music during the remainder of the day. The houses were very tastefully decorated, and the parochial officers, holding gold-headed staves, kept back people. A profusion of bunting was displayed; there was an illumination at night, and other evidences of the pleasure the good people of Watford felt at the honour done them by their beloved Queen."

The good people of Watford may have been less amused to note in *The Times* article the comment that "the only place of any importance on the route [was] St Albans".

1   In relating this version I am grateful to the www.stortfordhistory.co.uk website for allowing me to use their account of the execution as taken from *Twenty Centuries of England, Being the Annals of Bishops Stortford* by W. Basil Worsefold. I have cut and paraphrased certain sections.

2   Saunders, *History of Watford* (1931)

3   See www.stortfordhistory.co.uk/thorley/hadham_hall.html for a more detailed account of Capel.

The Parish Church

The life and governance of Watford revolved around and within the parish church of St Mary in Church Street. The wealth of local records and the essentially unaltered nature of the building enable us to obtain snapshots of life and death in Watford, certainly from the 12th century to the present day. St Mary's is one of only two Grade I listed buildings remaining in Watford. Believed to date from 1230, but certainly of earlier origins, St Mary's has been admired throughout Watford's recorded history. It is still an impressive and very much a living centre of Watford.

There are numerous descriptions of the church dating back to the end of the 17th century, which in their detail indicate a keen interest in the architecture of the building. There is a consistency in the descriptions of the interior of the building until a few notable changes were made at the end of the 19th century and

the beginning of the 20th century.

The church is almost certainly of Norman origin, although the earliest remaining parts date from 1230. A broken, carved stone Norman font was discovered and removed to St James's Church in Bushey during renovations in 1871, and is evidence of earlier origins. During the renovations 12th-century stones were found embedded in the fabric.

Further evidence of an earlier foundation is that the abbot of St Albans, Richard D'Albini, entertained King Henry I and the queen Matilda in 1115, at which time the king granted to St Alban's Abbey, amongst other baubles, the town of Watford and its market. The feast is described as being of great pomp and lasting for eleven days at the expense of the Abbey. In the same charter the church of Watford "to entertain strangers" is mentioned. A letter from Pope Clement III to Abbot Waring in 1188 refers to the income from the church at Watford. The vicarage is listed as being worth £12 per annum in 1291, and by the twenty-sixth year of

46. St Mary's, parish church of Watford, in 1905.

the reign of Henry VIII £21.12s.1d. per annum. By 1650 it is worth £50 per annum, and in 1870 the value of the living was £750 pa.

The church is of Early English style. The Chancel dates from around 1230, and the Nave about 1460. The altar is Jacobean and to the left of this is a brass plaque commemorating the marble steps given by Louisa, wife of the 6th Earl of Essex. The St Katherine's Chapel, now called the Heydon Chapel, is *c.*1500, and is believed to stand on the site of a 13th-century chantry founded by Petronel de Amville. The pulpit was once thought to have been by Grinling Gibbons, who worked nearby at Cassiobury, but the records show that it was erected in 1714 by Richard Bull. The Essex Chapel, the mortuary chapel of the Earls of Essex, was built on the site of the original Sacristy or Vestry by Bridget, widow of Sir

47. (left) The 15th-century tower was renovated in 1871.

48. (below) Interior of the church looking towards the Heydon Chapel on the far right. (Photo 2005)

49. The exquisitely carved monument to Sir Charles Morrison in the Essex Chapel. He died in March 1599, aged 51. (Photo 2005)

Richard Morrison, and Francis, 2nd Earl of Bedford in 1595. The two Morrison monuments in the Essex Chapel were built by the celebrated sculptor Nicholas Stone who agreed in a very specific contract, dated "3d day of March, 1628" with Dame Mary Morrison "of Kashbury" to undertake the work. Stone concludes the contract describing himself as a "Carver and Tombe Maker".

Chauncy, writing at the end of the 17th century, describes the Heydon Chapel as built by William Heydon of New Street, Watford, and Johanna his mother, which was known as the Chapel of St Katherine.

An 1880 description of the church applies with barely a few exceptions now.[1]

"This Church is deservedly celebrated for the number and splendour of its monuments especially those in the mortuary chapel of the Morrison and Essex families, in which is a grand old tomb to the memory of Sir Charles Morrison, Knight of Cashiobury, who died in March, 1599, aged 51. It has a canopy and pillars of various coloured marbles, under which is the effigy of Sir Charles in white marble, beautifully sculptured. He has a Vandyke beard, and a large ruff round his neck; and is represented in a reclining position in armour, with a helmet placed behind his legs; at each end of the tomb is a figure kneeling, which represent his son and daughter...."

50. (Above) Sir Charles Morrison's tomb (see below) in the Essex Chapel, showing his daughter kneeling to the left.

51. (Below) The magnificent Nicholas Stone monument to Sir Charles Morrison, who died in August 1628 aged 41. The figure to the foreground is his wife.

On the opposite side is another monument to Sir Charles Morrison, Bart. (son of the above), who died in August, 1628, aged 41, and to his wife also [ill. 51]. It is in its general form, similar to the one just described, but somewhat more elaborate. The figures of the baronet and his lady are both exquisitely sculptured. He is represented in armour, reclining on his right side, resting on his elbow, and his hand placed on a scroll. The lady reclines on a double cushion, and has a very handsome dress of the period, beautifully carved in all its details; the folds of her drapery are most gracefully arranged. On a lower stage are the figures of a youth and a boy kneeling and on the opposite side a young lady kneeling, with flowing drapery.

In the middle of the chapel are two large table monuments; the one to the east is to the memory of Bridget, Dowager Countess of

52. *The Essex Chapel, from John Britton's* History of Cassiobury, *1837. Note the Bedford monuments in the middle, which have now been removed to Chenies.*

53. *The Essex Chapel in 2005.*

Bedford, who died in 1600, aged 75; she had three husbands, the first of whom was Sir Richard Morrison. Her figure is in alabaster, well sculptured, in a reclining position, on the top of the tomb; she is elaborately dressed with a close cap and coronet on her head, and a large cloak, there is a square projection on the tomb, and a half-sized figure in armour on each side is kneeling on a cushion.

The other large central monument on the west side, is to the Lady Dame Elizabeth Russell, the wife of William Lord Russell, and "daughter and sole heire of Henrie Longe, of Shingay, in the countie of Cambridge". She died in June, 1611, aged 43; her dress has formerly been painted, and at her feet is a coronet and a lion...   Two monumental tablets against the south wall, record the memory of the Hon. John Forbes, son of the Earl of Granard, who died in March, 1796, aged 82, and his wife, Mary Forbes, daughter of William, third Earl

of Essex. On the floor of the chapel are three brass figures, inlaid in a large stone, inscribed to Henry Dickson, George Miller, and Anthony Cooper, late servants of Sir Charles Morrison.... Amongst other memorials to the Capel family in the chapel, is a mural monument to the memory of George fifth Earl of Essex, who died April 23rd, 1839, in his 81st year; it has a coronet and scroll, and coat of arms beautifully sculptured. Another tablet is to Harriet, the daughter of George, fifth Earl of Essex, who died May 14th, 1837, aged 29.

A visitor now would notice that the monuments in the middle of the Essex Chapel are no longer there. Those to the Dowager Countess of Bedford and Lady Elizabeth Russell made their final journeys to the Bedford family chapel at Chenies, Buckinghamshire in 1907. A memorial stone underneath the carpet in the chapel records this. After the removal of the founder's tomb the chapel remained derelict until it was

54. *Possibly the effigy of Lady Katherine Rotheram, d. 1625, in the Essex Chapel. The effigy has also been listed as being that of Lady Bridget, wife of Francis, Earl of Bedford, Dorothy Morrison who died in 1618, or an 'unknown' lady. The style of dress is of the 1580s*

restored in 1916 by Adela, Dowager Countess of Essex, in memory of her husband, the 7th Earl.

THE BELLS

Records of 1415 indicate the presence of bells in the church. A hundred years later there were five bells plus a 'Market Bell' used to signal the opening of the market. An inventory of 1553 included "5 bells in the steeple and one market bell". In 1610 a special preacher was appointed to address the people of Watford prior to market trading. Records of 1638 mention six bells in the church tower.

The 18th-century Vestry records note a number of problems with the church bells:

> June, 1704 – "The Great Bell have broke down and all her crown cannon broken off and that she cannot be hung up without being new cast and the Fifth Bell being not tuneable to the rest of the said bells, we do agree that the said two bells be not runn at the public charge." Nine present at this Vestry.

> September, 1704. – "Thomas Ewin, having paid £74. 17s. for new casting two of the bells he shall be paid the same and receive the approbation of the inhabitants of the town." Fifteen present at this vestry.

> 1750. "Whereas the Great Bell of this Parish is broke and the other bells are very bad and out of tune we do hereby consent that the six bells shall be taken down and new run and that there shall be an addition of metal to make a complete peal of 8 bells, the tenor to weigh 22cwt."

This resulted in action, for new bells were cast at the Whitechapel Foundry by Thomas Lester, and hung. One of the bells in the tower is said to bear the following inscription: "I to the church the living call, and to the grave I summons all. Thomas Lester, of London, made us all, 1750."

THE ORDNANCE SURVEY

St Mary's church tower was used in the early 19th century by surveyors for the Ordnance Survey:

> "....a temporary observatory was built on the leads of the tower, reaching to the vane, which was an object of considerable curiosity, and by the kindness of those engaged in the survey several inhabitants were allowed to ascend to this lofty building, from which a magnificent view of the surrounding country was obtained, especially when a telescope was used.'[2]

A CASE FOR HEALTH AND SAFETY

Henry Williams, writing in the late 1870s, describes an unfortunate event which probably took place in the first half of the 19th century. Always one for noting the darker aspects of the human condition he relates what occurred in St Mary's when a vault within the building was opened for a burial. Which one, he doesn't say.

> "Under the floor of the church, especially the nave, are the vaults of many of the gentry who resided at Watford; and that in the Essex cemetery, in which the Earls of Essex and families have been buried, contains many divisions one above the other, with oven-shaped openings into which the coffins were pushed and the mouths covered with a stone slab. A rather serious accident once happened when one of the vaults in the nave was opened for a burial. An old woman, named Nanny Fenson, who resided in one of the old cottages near the church, descended the steps of the vault to look at the coffins already there, and when on the last step, thinking she was at the bottom of the vault, she stepped forward and fell headlong into it, cutting her head badly against the edge of one of the coffins. The steps did not reach to the bottom of the vault by 3 or 4 ft. and there being very little light at the bottom, the poor old woman could not see when descending the steps the danger she was running into."

RENOVATION AND RESTORATION

The interior of the church was renovated in 1848 by Sir George Gilbert Scott. Various pillars and arches, which were beginning to fail, were strengthened. The galleries in the church were removed at this time.

"...the re-arrangement of the sittings on the ground floor gave many more seats... A handsome high carved oak screen was erected round St Katharine's Chapel, and the Essex Chapel was also enclosed with an oak screen, in which are inserted large panes of glass. The chancel is separated from the nave by a dwarf screen with gates of carved oak; there are seats for the choir and six stalls on each side of the chancel..."[3]

Deficiencies of the organ are reported in the mid 19th century:

"In the middle of [the] gallery towards the back stood the organ [not the present organ]....it then had a barrel arrangement in addition to the keys, and this was sometimes used when the organist was absent, one of the choristers turning the handle. He was not always successful in keeping time with the congregation, and would sometimes put a little speed on, thinking he was slow; but to his discomfiture he found he was already fast, and the extra turn or two brought him quite a bar before the congregation, and caused considerable confusion for a short time."[4]

Another description in the middle of the 19th century reveals that:

"On one side of the organ were rows of seats for the Free School boys and on the other similar seats for the girls of the same school. The wind was blown into the organ from the back, and here several lads would congregate with the blower, also a lad, and spend their time in cracking nuts and eating oranges, throwing the peels at the girls sitting near them."[5]

The writer continues with a description that demonstrates the class structure in attendance at church.

"Under the gallery were tiers of seats for the inmates of the workhouse and the poorer classes, and the christening pew was also here with its marble font and bell-shaped cover of panelled and carved oak. There were galleries over both north and south aisles; that over the north aisle extending from the tower to the Essex Cemetery, [note that at this time the Essex Chapel had yet to be consecrated] and that over the south aisle also from the tower to the east end of the edifice; they were approached by wide staircases near the tower, and narrow ones near the chancel arch... some of the pews in these galleries were entirely enclosed on three sides, forming comfortable rooms of fair dimensions, and were furnished with chairs and tables, and I am told that two or three centuries ago they contained stoves, with fire irons, coal scuttles, and hearth brushes. The fronts of these pews were about 3 ft. high, the book-board being covered with velvet or cloth, and, as viewed from the body of the church, were very much like the boxes in a theatre. The pew belonging to the Earls of Essex was erected in the arch dividing the chancel from the cemetery of the family, and was entered from the cemetery by a winding staircase. It was large, and extended 3 or 4 ft. into the chancel, the front having red curtains hanging on brass rails with handsome standards. This pew the Queen Dowager occupied when she resided at Cassiobury. The pews on the ground floor were very high, so that when the congregation were sitting or kneeling they could not be seen, and when standing only their heads were visible. They were capital places for indulging in a nap when the sermon was not brilliant, and not unfrequently did some of the congregation doze during the services, and now and then a hearty snore might be heard, or a thump against the boards of the pew when the sleeper was suddenly awakened. In these pews people indulged freely in eating apples, nuts, and oranges, and often a shovelful of rind and nutshells was swept from them by the pew cleaner. The church was heated by two immense stoves, each holding several scuttles of coals; one in the middle aisle and the other near the altar, the large iron pipes from which were supported by iron bars and carried through the walls near the roof. These fires were lit at seven o'clock each Sunday morning, and often had to be replenished during the services, great difficulty being experienced during cold weather in keeping the church warm... the boys often skirmished for the seat nearest the fire, and there were occasions when one boy pushed another from the seat on to the floor when he

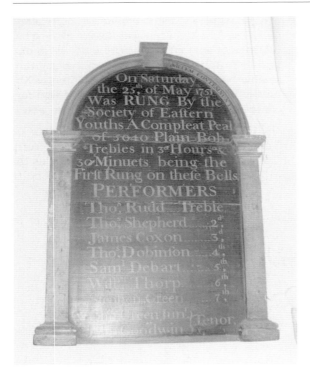

On Saturday
the 25th of May 1751
Was RUNG By the
Society of Eastern
Youths A Compleat Peal
of 5040 Plain Bob
Trebles in 3 Hours &
30 Minuets being the
First Rung on these Bells
PERFORMERS
Tho' Rudd   Treble
Tho' Shepherd   2d
James Coxon   3d
Tho' Dobinson   4th
Sam' Debart   5th
W.m Thorp   6th
    Green   7th
    Green Jun' Tenor
    Goodwin

55. *Plaque in St Mary's commemorating the first peal rung on Thomas Lester's bells in 1751.*

would not move from the coveted place. People were not so well behaved in church fifty years ago [in the 1830s] as now, the boys especially, who gave the beadle considerable trouble, and it was not unusual to hear loud talking in some of the pews, or the crack of the beadle's cane on the head of some troublesome urchin."[6]

An extensive restoration was undertaken in 1871 which included facing the exterior with flint and battlements on the 100ft high 15th-century tower. The work cost £6,839. 8s 5d and while it was going on an iron church was erected for prayer in the churchyard. The building also needed extensive underpinning as the foundations in the area of the tower and south wall were found to be giving way. At one stage, the workmen had a lucky escape when a wall collapsed, bringing down a section of the roof.

1   *A Guide to Hertfordshire, with a History and Description of the Various Towns and Villages* (1880)
2   Williams pp59, 60
3   *Ibid* p54
4   *Ibid* p48
5   *Ibid* p48
6   *Ibid* p49

Tales of St Mary's Churchyard

For centuries, churchyards were a centre of activity in village or town, where traders sometimes set up shop, and where people met and gossiped. It is recorded that "in the middle of the fourteenth century there was a recluse living in the churchyard of St Mary named Katherine Talemache who received a licence to beg from Bishop Bek."[1] In the fifteenth century there was a chapel in the churchyard to which Thomas Dutton left money

> "yerely to distribute and geve in the capell of Our Lady within the churchyarde of Watford on Maundy Thursday at the washing of the awters thirteen pennyloves to pore people in the worship of God and his xii apostles, and the two wardens yerely to restrayne in their handes for their diligent labor for the executing their office

to eche of them vid., the residue of the profettes yerely to be had of the said Bakers Acre to be delivered and paid by the said wardens to the use profette and mayntenaunce of the bretherhed masse of the Trinitie and Corpus Xti in the parish church of Watford aforesaid for ever."[2]

In 1772, the churchwardens obtained an Act to enlarge the churchyard. We have a description of the area prior to this which tells us that a road ran through the churchyard by the belfry door and "out near the Free School, and the ground on the right in front of the eight almshouses was a piece of greensward, in the middle of which was a well, from which the occupants of the almshouses obtained their water."

This was the piece obtained for the enlargement of the churchyard; part of it was converted into a public road, and the rest enclosed with a wall and merged into the churchyard.[3]

56. Plaque outside St Mary's Church, opposite the almshouses: 'A flint lined well probably dating from the middle or late Medieval Ages was discovered at this location in September 1999 during the Town Centre Enhancement works.'

57. The Clutterbuck family tomb in St Mary's churchyard, with the Free School in the left-hand background.

THEM DRY BONES

As part of the works to restore the church in 1871, it was decided, at a cost of £230, to lower the level of the churchyard, for in order to enter the church one needed to descend three or four steps – over the years burials had heightened the churchyard level, resulting in damp penetrating the church. During the work human remains were exposed:

> "It was hardly possible to remove a spadeful of earth without turning up human bones, and their exhumation caused some disapprobation amongst the parishioners, who spoke openly upon the subject, observing that it was a shocking thing to disturb the remains of the dead. This feeling rose to great indignation when many of the lads of the town were seen carrying about some of the bones that had been turned up..."[4]

Henry Williams, writing twelve years after, cannot resist detailing the more ghoulish sights:

> "Nearer the west end of the church is a vault which it was found necessary to lower, and when this was done the remains of a man who

had been buried in a winding-sheet were noticed; the sheet had given way from the face, showing the whiskers and the hair in a good state of preservation, although the body had been buried more than a hundred years."

By then the overcrowded burial ground had been closed and a new cemetery opened in Vicarage Road in 1858.

THE LEGEND OF THE FIG TREE

A legend developed about a tomb standing underneath the south wall of the Heydon Chapel through which a fig tree is supposed to have grown and bloomed annually. An atheist had said that after her death, should a fig tree grow out of her heart, then there was indeed a God. It did, or so it at first appeared, and her tomb became a major attraction during the 18th and 19th centuries, as undisputed evidence that a God existed. Visitors would attempt to remove and take leaves, twigs and branches as souvenirs A different version appears in the *Parish Magazine* of September 1898:

"Ben Wangford as he was generally called lived about the middle of the last century [1750s]. I can't say if he was a native of Watford or if married. But he was buried in St Mary's Churchyard and had a handsome tomb for that period. He was a man of enormous size, it is said that his boots could contain a bushel of corn. He did not believe in a hereafter state and wished, when buried, to have something placed with his remains that would germinate and then his relations would know that his soul was alive. If nothing appeared they might know that his opinion was correct. I have not heard what was placed in the coffin, but a fig tree appeared and for years was passed unnoticed by strangers. Now it is very much talked of, and people travel miles to visit the tomb."

Williams, commenting on the lowering of the churchyard observes that:

"When the churchyard was lowered an opportunity accidentally presented itself for a peep into this vault, and those who embraced that opportunity clearly saw that the root of the tree was not in the vault, but in the crown of the arch, 4 or 5 feet above where the lady's heart must have been. A few of the tendrils of the root had found their way through the brickwork of the arch and had attached themselves to the bottom of the vault, and to this probably may be attributed its luxuriant growth, as much more moisture must be obtained by these tendrils than the parts of the root attached to the crown of the arch. The peculiar shape of the coffin in which the lady was buried attracted attention also; it had a projection at the top, which led to the conclusion that the person must have died with her knees up, and that after death her legs could not be straightened.'[5]

An old inhabitant, attempting to date the origins of the fig tree in 1880, stated that he believed it to be at least 100 years old "as some fifteen or sixteen years ago I inquired of one of the oldest inhabitants what knowledge he had of its age, and he told me he remembered that when he was quite a child it was growing there, and apparently as large as now." The tree died from a severe frost in the 1960s.

58. *The fig tree tomb surrounded by railings, from a postcard c.1906.*

INVASION OF THE BODY SNATCHERS

For much of the 18th century and the first thirty years of the 19th century, body snatching was a lucrative occupation. Medical schools required corpses for dissection but were able to obtain these only from the gallows. In an age that firmly believed in resurrection and that dissection hindered or prevented this, only the bodies of criminals became available for such a final punishment. This shortage was partly alleviated on the passing of the infamous Anatomy Act of 1832 whereby it was permitted to use the bodies of those who had died alone in workhouses and which were unclaimed. This had the advantage to the parish that it could sell the body and not have to pay for a pauper's burial.

However, before that, the nearer to a medical school the churchyard lay, the greater the risk of a premature resurrection. Numerous churchyards in the vicinity of London bear witness to the fear of the so-called 'resurrectionists'. Many tombs were extensively railed around, or else, where the family could afford it, a watch was put on the new burial to protect it. The winter was considered most dangerous since the cold preserved the corpses for a longer period. Henry Williams wrote:

"Watford has been notorious for body-snatching, and this shameful desecration was carried on here up to about thirty-five years ago; and so great was the fear of persons who had lost relatives that they would be torn from their graves by some ruthless desecrator, that extraordinary means were adopted to prevent it. The newly-raised mounds were marked and watched for several days and even nights, until it was thought decomposition would stop the removal of the body. This watching was generally resorted to by poor persons, as the better-to-do class generally had a slab of oak laid on the top of the coffin, and secured by crosspieces of wood, let into holes made in the sides of the graves. I remember being present, when a boy, at a funeral, and staying to see the oak slab fixed down... on another occasion, when a gentleman named Ewer died suddenly in Chalk Hill Lane in 1845, his relatives went to the trouble and expense of having three leaden

coffins removed from the family grave and his body placed underneath, in order to secure it against the depredations of body-snatchers.'[6]

Watford's notoriety is further confirmed by Henry Lomas, a plumber who lived and died in Watford and who kept a diary between January 1822 and February 1828. His entry for the 25th March 1822 observes:

"The Body of a young Girl was taken from the Watford Church Yard. It was made into a parcel about 3 feet by 1 foot and after the wretches had had it about at different Public Houses it was booked to go to Town by the Hempstead Coach. Some persons having suspicion they were resurrection Men searched the Parcel and found it to contain the Body [of] a human Being. They then took out the Corpse and having put something else in its stead dispatched a constable with it to apprehend the Person who came for it. The man who came was not the same who booked it but an accomplice. He was taken into custody, brought to Watford and then committed to St Albans Gaol to take his trial at the Sessions."

On the 18th April 1822:

"At St Albans sessions the Resurrection Man who took the Girl from Watford church yard was found guilty and sentenced to pay a fine of £20 and to be imprisoned for two years.'[7]

1   *Victoria County History*, Hertfordshire, Vol. 2 p466
2   *Ibid*, p466
3   Williams p63
4   *Ibid* p61
5   *Ibid* p64
6   *Ibid* p65
7   Knight, Judith, and Flood, Susan, *Two Nineteenth Century Hertfordshire Diaries* p27 (2002)

The Vicars of St Mary's

It tended to be the younger sons of the aristocracy that went into the clergy. The incumbent received a comfortable income without too much disruption to his lifestyle, which usually involved the pleasures and privileges of the landed classes. There is a full list of the vicars of St Mary's dating from 1309 to the present day on two plaques mounted on a wall of the church, just before reaching the Essex Chapel. A few have left more than their names to remember. The following come from the records of *The old Archdeaconry of St Albans.*

1584. Mr Henry Edmonds, vicar, no graduate, nor preacher resident; of honest life and conversation; value of benefice £21 12s., whereout goeth a pension of £8 a year. Patron, the Earl of Bedford.

1599. Articles exhibited against Henry Baldwyn, Wm. Edlyn, Wm. Swift, and Christopher Gibson, churchwardens of Watford, for neglect of duty in not presenting to the Court their Vicar Anthony Watson for certain disorders. That the said Anthony Watson since Easter, 1599, has not read the Queen's injunction, nor has he for the space of two years last past read the Commination on Ash Wednesday: in the saying of Public Prayer and administration of the Sacraments he hath not worn or used the surplice: hath received the Communion himself standing and administered the same to divers persons, some standing, some sitting in very confused manner: he hath refused or omitted to use the sign of the Cross in baptism; and for 20 Sundays and holy days hath omitted in the Church to read distinctly and reverently the Common Prayers and other Divine Service: and on Wednesdays and Fridays hath refused or omitted to repair to the Church and give warning to the people by the 'noleing of a bell' and to read the litanye and prayers. And likewise in his sermons at divers

and sondrie times and in his prayers omitted and refused to give her Majesty her usual title, Queen of England and France, Defender of the Faythe, & c. And in marriage hath omitted to use the ringe and to catechize the children of the said parish. And the said Mr. Anthony Watson in his sermons and public exercises in the said church at Watford hath inveighed publicly against the rites and ceremonies to be used in this Church of England with a disliking of the same and hath said that the said rites and ceremonies are not agreeable to the Word of God and that the Church of England is more polluted with traditions and ceremonies than all the Churches of Christiendom where the gospel is preached and that the article in the Crede concerning Christ's descension into hell was foisted in by some Baptists.

It was the churchwardens who were penalised:

1599 Order of Penance enjoined to Henry Baldwyn, Wm. Edlyn, and Christopher Gibson, churchwardens of Watford, for not presenting divers faults concerning the neglect of their Minister in divers things by him to be done and their faults by him committed. The said churchwardens shall upon Sundays next immediately after the ende of Evening Prayer in the chancel of the church of Watford before six of honester parishioners confess their faults and defects by their minister done, committed and omitted, punishable by the Ecclesiastical censures, which they did know of and as appeareth by their several answers made to the articles administered against them in this Court. And shall know themselves very penitent for the same, desiring God to forgive them and promising hereafter to be more careful in the executing and doing their offices.

It was not long before Watford found itself at the mercy of a rather more devious vicar, by the name of Cornelius Burgess. He occupied the living from 1618 to 1644 at which time he was ejected by Parliament. He appears to have been an opportunist. He supported the Royalist cause and Charles I until it appeared that the king might not be the winning party. He bought and sold church lands and remarkably wrote the none-too-subtly titled tracts: *No Sacrilege nor Sin to alien or purchase the Lands of Bishops and others whose Offices are abolished*, followed by, *The Lawfulness of buying Bishop's Lands*, and finally, if only to further justify his activities, an *Apology for Purchases of Lands, late of Bishops, Deans, and Chapters*. Unfortunately for Cornelius Burgess, he fell out with his Parliamentarian friends who ejected him from Watford in 1644. In a document titled 'Accounts of Plundered Ministers, 6 February 1644-5' it was ordered "...that Cornelius Burges Dr. in Divinity doe deliver up unto Philip Goodwin minister of Watford in the County of Hertford all Keyes of and belonging to the Vicarage house of Watford aforesaid or doe shew good cause to the contrary thereof before this Committee." With the restoration of Charles II in 1660, Burgess was forced to hand back the Church lands, and he retired in extreme penury to Watford where he died on 6th June 1665. He is buried in St Mary's.

A NOTORIOUS VICAR

There is something of the Toad of Toad Hall about the Honourable and Reverend William Robert Capel, Vicar of St Mary's from 1799. He is variously described as nephew or half brother to the 5th Earl of Essex, but one abbreviated biography describes him as the second son by the second wife of the 4th Earl of Essex. He was, however, the half-brother to the 5th Earl, and half-uncle to the 6th Earl. As well as being Vicar of Watford, he was also, from 1805, the Rector of Rayne in Essex, and from 1814, Chaplain to the Sovereign. Born 1775, he married Sarah, only daughter of Samuel Salter of Rickmansworth in 1802. His tenure at Watford lasted from 1799 until his death in 1854. This span brought him within the memory of a number of Watford inhabitants who put pen to paper during the latter part of the 19th century. Capel, as well as tending to matters spiritual was also Master of the Old Berkeley Hunt. This led to a legal dispute with the 5th Earl, when having been specifically ordered not to hunt over the Earl's land, on 1 April 1809 at Cassiobury, he proceeded to do just that.[1]

He was described by Josiah Conder, a resi-

dent of Watford Field Place from 1824 to 1839, as "generally to be seen on a fine day, with his portly figure, white trousers, and jovial face, chatting with his parishioners; or not seldom, in the hunting season, riding through the street in his scarlet jacket and white cords."[2]

Henry Williams in 1884 paints a marvellous picture of the aristocratic vicar:

"The Hon. and Rev. W. Capel, the late Vicar of Watford, was a gentleman of some notoriety, and there were not wanting men uncharitable enough to construe some of his acts into faults which ought not to be found in a minister of the gospel. He was an ardent sportsman, and having the coverts of Cassiobury to shoot over, was often seen with his dog and gun, when, in the opinion of some people, he should have been ministering to the wants of his parishioners. He was a magistrate, and no friend to poachers who abounded in his day. They were a bold and villainous set of fellows, but they found in him one who had courage to confront them and unmask their nocturnal depredations. More than once he was seen to stop a poacher at early morn in Cassiobury Park, and search his pockets for the game he was sure to find there. When any one of these fellows was summoned for poaching, it was a relief for him to know he was not to be tried by Mr. Capel, who generally inflicted the fullest penalty for the offence. I remember following a poacher down the street, who was going to be tried for poaching. A friend met him, to whom he said, 'Do you know if Old Billy Capel is going to hear my case?' His friend answered, 'He is.' 'Then,' said the poacher, 'I shall get it hot.' Kind and charitable in every other respect , his name was often found at the head of a subscription list for the relief of the poor, and he was ever willing to help in the formation or management of any institution that had for its object the good of his parishioners... Outwardly, he appeared to look upon the service of the church only as a matter of form; he read quickly, and preached short sermons, and the schoolboys used to rejoice when he conducted the service alone, as they knew they would get out of church early. More than once I heard persons remark when they saw the congregation leaving church early, 'I know who preached this morning!'.... His frank and open manner indicated a levity that he really did not possess; but he was a a man who did not consider religion was intended to make men's pleasures less, provided those they indulged in were harmless.... He was fond of hearing the news of the town, and when the beadle attended him in the vestry to change his surplice before the sermon, he would ask, 'Well, Dick, what's the news to-day?' and if that functionary had no news to tell him he would say, 'You are a poor newsmonger.' He was fond of billiards, and was a member of a subscription billiard room at the Essex Arms Hotel, which room then stood on part of the site of the present Corn Exchange. A conversation between him and a lady was talked freely of in the town. The lady ventured to express to him her opinion that killing game and playing billiards were not quite proper things for a minister to indulge in, when he replied, 'My dear madam, game is provided by God for our use, and we cannot eat it while it is flying about; and as to playing billiards, I never bet when I play a game, or swear when I lose one.' The lady shook her head on leaving him, apparently unconvinced by his argument. It was also said that a gentleman once spoke to him upon the same subjects; the

vicar argued with him, but failing to win him over to his view of the case, he said, 'If you think I do wrong, don't do as I do, but do what I tell you when I am in the pulpit.' He lived esteemed by his parishioners, and his death was a source of sorrow to all but the poachers, who rejoiced that so formidable an enemy had been removed from amongst them.'[3]

Capel's lack of impartiality as a magistrate warranted a comment in Henry Lomas's diary. The entry for 17th August 1826:

"Two Boys of tender years named Winfield and Taylor were committed to St Albans Gaol for one month by Mr Wm Capel for being found fishing in the tumbling bay ditch[4] and on the following day I suppose finding himself in error ordered them to be liberated. To stop legal proceedings against him he gave the Boys a Guinea each."

1   Ball, Alan William, *Street and Place Names in Watford* p28 (1973)
2   Conder, Eustace R and Conder, Josiah: *A Memoir* pp239-241 (1857)
3   Williams pp 57, 58
4   An area of the Colne, south-west of Watford.

Getting about

OVERCROWDING ON THE STAGE COACH

"*Gilbert Claydon,* the driver of the Bicester stage-coach, was convicted before the Earl of Essex, and the Sitting-Magistrate, at Watford, Herts, in the penalty of six pounds, for carrying four persons on the roof of his coach above the number allowed by the Act of the 28th George III." *The Times,* 9 October 1794

Overcrowding *and* speeding were taken seriously, it seems. The following article in *The Times* of 29 August 1818 suggests that coaches were capable of achieving greater speeds along

59. Item from The Times *of 27 October 1786 relating to bad conduct by coachmen.*

On Monday laſt came on to be tried, at the Seſſions-houſe, on Clerkenwell-green, an indictment againſt John Greenway, the driver of the Watford ſtage coach, and ſome of the proprietors of the ſame, for aſſaulting and wilfully driving the leaders of the fore horſes of the ſaid ſtage to and againſt the mare of John Clements, of Wimpole-ſtreet, Cavendiſh-ſquare, Eſq. as Mr. Clements was riding in company with another Gentleman, and their ſervants, on the Paddington-road, in the month of July laſt; when the cauſe was called on, Mr. Fielding, counſel for the defendant, propoſed to Mr. Clements, that the defendant ſhould pay the coſts, and ſign any kind of apology Mr. Clements ſhould think proper, which propoſal Mr. Clements refuſed acceding to, declaring, at the ſame time, that he did not come there with any perſonal reſentment againſt the defendant, but that he cauſed the proſecution to be carried on for the good of ſociety, and whatever the event might be, he ſhould be doing nothing more than diſcharging that duty which every man owed the public. The cauſe then went on, and after a long and impartial hearing, the defendant was found guilty, and the Court very judiciouſly ordered him to be impriſoned for three months in Priſon.

We hope the above example will be a proper check and warning to the brethren of the whip, and at the ſame time recommending the ſame laudable conduct to be followed by every gentleman, which would totally ſubdue the arrogance of coachmen in general.

the Edgware Road than can modern-day traffic:

"Mr. Jonathan Goodall, one of the proprietors and drivers of the Watford stage-coach, also appeared to summons, on an information laid against him by one of the passengers in the coach, charging him with having, on the 8th instant, carried fourteen outside his coach, not being licensed to carry more than twelve outside passengers. The Magistrates convicted the defendant in the full penalty of 40l. for the two passengers so over-carried… There was a second information against the same defendant, charging him with wantonly and furiously driving his horse along the Edgware-road, on the day mentioned in the first information, at the rate of 14 miles an hour, his coach being at the time heavily laden, whereby he endangered the lives of his Majesty's subjects. The case being proved, the magistrates, being determined, if possible, to put an end to this dangerous practice, convicted the defendant in the further sum of 10/."

In 1786 the driver of the Watford Stage was sentenced to three months imprisonment for reckless driving *(ill. 59).*

STAGING POSTS

A journey to London by stage coach took four hours. There were two coaches daily in each direction leaving from the Essex Arms, Rose & Crown, Green Man and the George. An almost romantic description by Eustace and Josiah Conder of Watford Field Place (1824-1839) describes their coming and going:

"Every night, the mail-coach, with its flaring eyes and red-coated guard, made the quiet streets echo to its horn, picked up, perhaps, its one passenger, and excited mysterious feelings of respect and wonder in the minds of little boys."

The last regular horse-drawn coach service through Watford was in 1886. An advertisement calls it the 'wonder coach'. The service operated between London and St Albans, leaving Hatchett's Hotel in Piccadilly at 10.45am, and arriving at the Rose & Crown in Watford at 12.50pm before setting off for the Peahen

60. *Watford's first motor bus, taken in Woodford Road, opposite the Trade Union Hall. The route taken was very much at the whim of the owner.*

Hotel in St Albans at 12.54 pm. The single fare was 10 shillings (50p) and a return ticket cost 15 shillings. The equivalent of first class travel was the 'Box Seat' for which a surcharge of two shillings and sixpence applied each way.

HORSE BUSES

In 1884 a horse-drawn bus ran between Croxley Green and Harrow, provided by the London & North Western Railway Co. In 1898 a service which was claimed to be the first commercial vehicle operation of its type in Watford, began. Operated by a Mr G Bence of 46 Grover Road, the bus ran between Bushey Arches and Callowland, a route which depended on the whims of Mr Bence, running variously via Queens Road, Clarendon Road or St Albans Road. As he himself proudly remarked, "the passengers had no say". The journey at a maximum speed of 10 mph took about 30 minutes and the fare was 3d. Despite an initial surge of interest, not surprisingly his potential passengers lost interest and the service was soon withdrawn.

THE GRAND JUNCTION CANAL

Canals had their heyday when roads for the transportation of heavy goods were poorly maintained, and before railways largely stole their trade. Work began on the Grand Junction Canal to connect the Midlands with the Thames and London Docks in May 1793, employing 3,000 men known as 'navigators' (navvies). It runs through Cassiobury Park. Before this the waterways linking Birmingham and London wound for a tortuous 269 miles, but the Grand Junction reduced this journey to 138 miles. Eventually, once the Regent's Canal had been

61. *The Canal with the lock keeper's cottage, c.1906.*

62. *The same view today, but the cottage has not survived.*

built, the Grand Junction connected directly with the docks at Limehouse, but before that was completed in 1820 goods were either offloaded on to lighters on the Thames at Brentford, or else on to carts at Paddington basin.

In 1929, following the merger of a number of companies the canal became known as the Grand Union Canal Company.

Inevitably canals suffered when the railways came. This was to be the fate of the Grand Union after the establishment of the London & Birmingham Railway which the canal company strongly opposed.[1]

THE RAILWAY ARRIVES
The London & Birmingham Railway (later renamed London & North Western) arrived at Watford Junction on the 26 July 1837, despite the objections of the Earls of Clarendon and Essex who saw this development as noisy, dirty and generally undesirable. It was to be a defining moment in the future progress of Watford from sleepy agricultural town, to an industrial centre. Josiah Conder, a resident of Watford during the 1830s, who published his memoirs in 1857, observed that 'everybody knows where

Watford is; for it is a station on the North-Western Railway, and everybody has travelled by the North-Western Railway… but thirty years ago everybody did not know where Watford was. Railways and locomotives were among the undeveloped possibilities of the future. Any one, who had talked of travelling from London to Birmingham in four hours, and of crossing the Atlantic in a week, would have been laughed to scorn as a hair-brained enthusiast…."

The original station was in St Albans Road, and this still remains as a Grade II listed building. It was constructed between 1836 and 1837 and was used by the Dowager Queen Adelaide in 1843 during her residence at Cassiobury House. A specially constructed covered entrance was installed for her use.

The Times on 24 August 1839 described the building:

"Passing onward through Primrose-hill and Kensal-green Tunnels, and Harrow, we arrive at Watford. At this station the tickets are collected from the passengers arriving by the up-trains from Birmingham. The station is fitted up with booking-office, passengers' room, ladies' waiting rooms (elegantly

63. The Colne Viaduct in September 1837.

64. *The original Watford Station still stands at 147a St Albans Road.*

65. *Watford Junction Station in 1860.*

furnished), inspector's room, porter's room, stationary engine house, with an engine of four-horse power used to throw water into the tank above for supplying the locomotive engines (on their requiring it) on their arrival at the station; a repairing house, fitted up with furnaces, lathes, and all necessaries for that department. The whole of the station is covered with a light corrugated iron roof...."

The station occupies a site where three small houses once stood, "one occupied by Mr. Poulton, a leather breeches and gaiter maker; and on the opposite side Mr Draycott, maltster, [who] had a yard in which a horse with blinkers used to go round under a beam to grind malt.'[2]

TROUBLE WITH THE NAVVIES

The 'navvies' who built the railway and the Watford tunnel were not highly regarded. A local resident writing in the 1870s bemoaned the early binge drinking and thuggery:

"How different was the navvy of 1838 from him of the present day. The former was looked upon with abhorrence because of his drunken and blackguardly conduct, while the men who follow the work of a navvy at the present day are mostly quiet, steady men, and respectable members of society. Although very young at the time the railway was made through Watford, I well remember the dreadful scenes frequently presented to the inhabitants. Scarcely a night passed without a drunken fight or a row at one of the public houses. The men were a terror to everybody, and respectable females were scarcely able to walk in the streets without meeting with some improper conduct from them. Black eyes and broken heads were the order of the day, and so daring were the navvies that the parish constables were really afraid of some of them. On one occasion a constable was overpowered by one of these fellows, and as soon as he was able to get away he ran for his life, followed by his adversary; he took refuge in the butcher's shop......'[3]

A number of navvies suffered in a tragic accident whilst building the Watford Tunnel.

An article in *The Times* of 12 November 1835 takes an early but sensible approach that if the working practices were to be improved, the loss of life would be reduced accordingly.

DANGER ON THE RAILWAY

It is sometimes forgotten that the early railway system was often dangerous. Almost immediately after the railway came to Watford accidents and legal cases seeking compensation for injury appear on a regular basis. Some of the early records of these accidents spare no details, giving melodramatic descriptions of the various forms of decapitation incurred. The result of delays, accidents, and the various indignities associated with early rail travel often led to the victim sending a letter to *The Times*. The following could be regarded as an early version of the 'leaves on the line' incident:

OFF THE RAILS IN 1839

"The mail train from London, which should have arrived at Stafford station yesterday morning (Friday), soon after 4 o'clock, did not make its appearance before half-past 7, in consequence of having run off the rails near Watford, through the negligence of the person whose duty it is to attend to the points misplacing those of the cross-rails. Fortunately, no person was injured, and the engine only partially damaged. Shortly after the accident occurred a messenger was sent to the Watford station for another engine, which caused a delay of an hour, and on its return that part of the train not off the rails was conveyed back to the Harrow station, a distance of six or seven miles, before it could be brought on the proper line for proceeding to Birmingham; the whole time lost was nearly three hours." (*The Times*, 12 Feb, 1839)

RAILWAY ACCIDENT. An unfortunate accident occurred on the London and North Western Railway, at the Watford station, between 2 and 3 o'clock this morning, to the engine-driver and fireman of a goods' train, arising from the heedlessness of the former. The first goods' train had been delayed on the

66. *From* The Times, *1 December 1851.*

road between Wolverton and Leighton, by the failure of power in the engine which drew it. From that station it was assisted to Tring by the second goods' train and thence to London (the road being an incline nearly the whole way), was allowed to proceed without further assistance, and stopped at Watford according to regulation. There the usual signals were exhibited to prohibit any other train from entering the station. The signals for caution were also exhibited by the policeman at each end of the tunnel, and the night being foggy there was additional reason for the enginemen of the second train (who were perfectly aware that the other could not be far ahead) to advance with the greatest care. Unhappily, this was not observed, and coming into collision with the train in front, the engineman and fireman of no. 72 engine had fractures of the legs. The poor fellows were, as early as

67. *From* The Times, *12 November 1835.*

possible, removed to the North London Hospital, and in one case, at least, amputation of the limb will be necessary.' (*The Times*, 1 October 1846)

BLOCKADE OF THE WATFORD TUNNEL

"Last Friday evening the train due at Aylesbury at 5 o'clock did not reach the town until 7. Much uneasiness, therefore, was the result, especially to those who expected friends at that time. When the train at last arrived, we were assured that no accident had happened

68. *Construction of the Watford Tunnel, a drawing dated 6 June 1837.*

to any human being, but that they had been detained at Watford for two hours, unable to proceed by reason of something wrong within the tunnel. A luggage train broke down within the tunnel, and was so completely smashed to pieces that two hours elapsed before a multitude of workmen could clear away the rubbish, and lines of carriages, extending a mile and a-half, awaited the opening of the passage. Railway officers are pledged to secrecy in such matters, and the policy of the directors is, as much as possible, to keep the world in the dark. Nothing, however, could be more alarming than the idea of such a calamity within a tunnel of so much extent. " (*The Times*, 12 Sep, 1853)

Fatal accidents, people being run down on the line both near and at Watford, become a more frequent occurrence after 1839 with the number of Coroners' Inquests increasing proportionately with the popularity of the railway. An item in *The Times* of 22 Jan 1840 reports a policeman who was "stationed at the London end of the Watford tunnel" being struck and killed by the Birmingham train.

THE UNDERGROUND ARRIVES

The Bakerloo line was the first Underground network line to reach Watford even if initially it used London & North Western Railway tracks. The LNWR had constructed a line alongside their main track as far as Watford High Street in February 1913. Plans for a suburban service to Euston fell through and the Bakerloo line was encouraged to extend their line from Paddington to Queen's Park and then, using the LNWR's new track, run trains on to Watford High Street, which opened on 16 April 1917.

It was left to the Metropolitan line to serve the western side of Watford. The Metropolitan Railway which ran from Baker Street to Aylesbury had opened in 1885, and an early plan was for a branch line north of Moor Park to be built, passing through Croxley and terminating at Watford. This project was shelved by the intervention of the First World War and it was not until 2 November 1925 that this branch line was opened, terminating at Cassiobury Park Avenue. Its construction included the viaduct over the river valley at Croxley.

WATFORD'S ROADS

The roads in and around Watford from medieval times to the eighteenth century were badly maintained and subject to the funding and energy of local parishes who used, on the whole, the unpaid labour of its residents. As wheeled traffic became more common, this system could not cope with the task, and as from the beginning of the eighteenth century a growing number of turnpike trusts were created with powers to collect tolls for the use of stretches of main roads in return for their repair and maintenance. Nearly 2,000 particular Turnpike Acts were enacted in that century until in 1773 a General Turnpike Act was passed which speeded up the whole process and took less of Parliament's time.

By 1765 there were two Turnpike Trusts in the Watford area: the Hatfield-Barnet Trust and the Sparrow Herne Trust from Bushey Heath to Aylesbury.

TOLL KEEPING

In 1850 the toll gate at Bushey Arches, now under the Wickes store, charged 6d for a horse and cart and 3d for a man on horseback. Tolls

The Times (ill. 69) not all toll-collectors were honest.

Of the tolls and toll-keepers we have been left one particularly graphic report:

"....the occupation of tollgate keeper was not an enviable one, especially at this gate... [bottom of the High Street]. How many times in a week the poor man was cursed, either for being too exact in demanding toll or not rising from his uneasy couch sufficiently quick in the night, cannot be told; but, like all tollgate keepers, he was looked upon by those who desired to pay as little as possible, or not to pay at all, as a contemptible wretch who wished to pick their pockets, and was treated accordingly."[4]

Even so, the surface of roads was still inadequate to deal with the amount of traffic and there are 19th-century reports in Watford of local residents dousing the High Street with water to keep down the dust. One in 1849 tells us that the roads in Watford were "unscientifically formed, and suffered to remain unscavenged [uncleaned], and thus to become rotten from wet. They are not drained. In the

CAUTION TO TOLL COLLECTORS.—The following case was tried before a bench of Magistrates at Watford, on Tuesday se'nnight :—William Clark, the toll-collector at the Hayden-lane-gate, near Watford, (on the Reading trust), was convicted in the full penalty of 5l., under an act of Parliament passed in the third year of the reign of his present Majesty for regulating turnpike-roads, for omitting to give a ticket to Mr. Perry, of Watford, and thereby obtaining the toll twice in one day, contrary to the provisions of the aforesaid act

69. *From* The Times, *26 July 1824.*

were the bane of everyday road users, and toll collectors ranked second only to stage-coach drivers in unpopularity. The users of roads into and out of Watford suffered accordingly, with the tollgate keepers acquiring a status similar to that of today's parking wardens. The toll-house stood at the bottom of the High Street near the railway bridge. Another toll-house stood at the northern end. As can be seen in

town they are in many places hollow..."[5] As is the case so many times where self-interest is involved it was noted that "the highway in front of the surveyors' houses [those responsible for the highway] was in far better order than elsewhere, and it seems to be admitted on all hands that this was a sort of legitimate perquisite of office.'[6] A report compiled by Sir James McAdam, of tar macadam fame, and a local

70. *An early photograph of the toll gate, Bushey Arches. The Gate was removed on 1 July 1872, but it is commemorated by a plaque in the wall of the Wickes Superstore now on the site.*

resident, says of the High Street that 'the paved water channels in many parts being higher than the centre of the turnpike road... so as effectually to prevent the surface water finding its way into the water channel.' In other words gravity was being asked to perform the impossible. In 1888 control of the roads was handed to the newly formed County Council.

1   Faulkner, Alan H, *The George & the Mary: a Brief History of the Grand Union Canal Carrying Company Ltd* (1973)

2   David Downer's recollections, 1916, quoted in Saunders

3   Williams, p112

4   *Ibid.* p72

5   G T Clark's report to the Board of Health, 1849

6   *Ibid*

The Colne and Floods

The Colne has been central to the development and history of Watford since prehistoric times. It was until fairly recent years a source of clean water from which the brewing industry developed, and provided the people of Watford with food, drink and recreation. Henry Williams recollects that at the Fighting Cocks public house, close to the river, was a pleasure-boat station belonging to Mrs Lucy Deacon. He writes that,

"one could hire a boat and enjoy a row up the river as far as Bushey Mill Bridge; the charge was one shilling per hour, and the person or party hiring the boat was required to leave half-a-crown with the landlady as a security against any loss she might sustain by damage done to her boat. The house and premises were generally crowded on Sunday afternoons and evenings, and not unfrequently a spill into the water occurred when the boat was occupied by youths who had indulged freely in drinking before they had started on their voyage up the Colne.'[1]

Williams also comments that so popular was the Colne as a source of leisure that private boxes had been erected along the side of the stream for bathing, similar to the bathing huts in England's seaside towns. The boxes were still present and being used in the 1880s.

SKATING AND FISHING

The Colne would often flood the locality and when it receded often the remaining water would freeze over allowing "thousands to indulge in the healthy pastime of skating." This took place in the area of Loates Lane Arch and a colourful description remains of tents being erected for the ladies to put on their skates, and leave articles of clothing. The ice was lit at night with torches, hopefully at a safe distance, and skating would take place for maybe two or three days before the ice would begin to crack.

In the 1830s the Colne at Watford was a fisherman's paradise, as it contained many varieties such as pike, trout and perch, but by the end of the 19th century unrestricted fishing led to the demise of the fish stock. In the 1850s a Mr. Jonathan King is credited with imposing a form of fisheries management, including restocking the Colne with trout. This is the same Jonathan King whom Henry Lomas describes in his diary entry of 6th December 1825 as "taking possession of Watford Place". King also gave his name to King Street. Williams wrote in 1883:

"At various times Mr. King put a quantity of Neuchatel trout in the stream, and some fine ones have been occasionally caught – one in April, 1883, by Mr. C.H. Thomas, of Colnebrook, weighing nine pounds and three quarters. In 1856, when there were plenty of fish in the Colne, Mr. King netted, at Wiggen Hall, fifty-four pounds of trout in one day. At one time the canal in Cassiobury Park was dragged periodically with a net, and a large quantity of fine fish caught, the best of which were sent as presents to some of the inhabitants of Watford. Mr. Mead has stated that the largest quantity of eels caught on any one day at Watford Mills was about three hundred-weight. Fish hatching was carried on at one time by Mr. Hibbert, Lord Essex, and Mr. J. King."[2]

FLOODING IN WATFORD

Thomas Baskerville on a visit in 1671 experienced a forerunner of the 1906 Watford flood:

"From Cassabell [Cassiobury] went to Watford, a market town... where the water was so high we could not well pass over it without wetting our saddles. For which reason we went another way to St Albans, a great market town about six miles from Watford." Thomas Baskerville, 24th September 1671.[3]

Things were not to improve:

"The waters have been out in most parts of the country to an alarming height. So great and forcible has been the rush of water on the Lee Bridge Road, that several Ladies have been afraid to pass in their carriages. The

71. *Watford Market Place after the Great Storm of 27 July 1906. Just one of the many recorded floods in Watford's history.*

Jew's Harp Bridge, on the road to Stanmore, is totally impassable, and at the lower part of Watford, the inhabitants have been absolutely obliged to reside in the upper stories. It is much to be feared that great quantities of cattle perished in the various marshes." *The Times*, 6 December, 1794

Henry Lomas comments in his diary that on 5 May 1822 there was "A tremendous storm of Thunder & rain. It fell in torrents so much as to completely inundate the lower part of Watford Town"

The better news appears on 6 June the same year:

"The Weather was this Month intensely Hot. It was said the thermometer never stood higher in this Country. It stood at 115 degrees in the Sun at five p.m. on Thursday the 20ᵗʰ Inst."

By the end of the 1830s and the arrival of the London to Birmingham railway, flooding was being blamed on the environmental disruption caused by the railway:

"The neighbourhood of Watford has alas been very much inundated, and the meadows extending nearly across to Barnet have within the last few days been covered with an immense sheet of water. The Birmingham railroad, which completely intersects this part of the country, had the effect of backing the water, and causing it to settle in this locality, the culverts not being sufficiently capacious to allow it a free passage, and the by-roads and lanes in the neighbourhood of Bushy and Watford were rendered completely impassable from the depth of the water." *The Times*, 4 Dec, 1839

On 18 January 1881 Watford was brought to a halt by a snow storm that forced several Watford residents to spend the night on a train which had come to a halt at Wembley.

1   Williams p96
2   *Ibid*
3   *Ibid* p24

Learning Places

In 1595 there is a reference in the Watford records to George Redhead "schoolmaster". A Free School in Watford is mentioned in 1640, when Francis Combes of Hemel Hempstead in his will dated 12 December 1641

> "charged all his Estate in Hempstead with an annual Payment of ten Pounds, for a Free-School in Watford, where poor Children are taught to cast Accompt, read English, and write."[1]

> "The master hath the use of a room over the two houses belonging to the Church estate nearest the churchyard, for the above purpose, rent free, and is also paid 13/4 a year out of the church rents for teaching an additional boy."

It has been suggested that the wording may mean that a school already existed. The next reference occurs in 1698 where poor people who dwell in cottages "under the school" are mentioned. All, however, did not go smoothly after Combes' demise and the Charity Commission was forced to intervene in 1650 as Sir Richard Combes had failed to pay the £10 p.a. for ten years. But in 1689 payments were again withheld and not resumed until the intervention of Chancery in 1709.

ELIZABETH FULLER'S FREE SCHOOL
Born in Tiverton, Devon in 1644, Elizabeth Fuller was following in a family tradition when she founded a school in Watford. She was born Elizabeth Chilcott into a family which had founded a free school in her home town. Fuller was three times widowed and it was on the death of her third husband that she devoted herself to the creation and support of the Watford Free School. The building now has a commercial use, but is still well preserved, overlooking St Mary's churchyard.

Nathaniel Salmon in 1727 described it as "...fine both within and without. In the School-Room, which is wainscoted, and hath a Chimney-Piece gilt and adorned, is the Picture of Mrs. Fuller in her Widow's Dress, sitting with

72. *Elizabeth Fuller.*

a Bible in her Hand." The building is typical of early Queen Anne architecture. The original inscription over the door remains:

> "Anno Dni 1704. This Free School was built and endowed for the teaching of poor children at the proper cost of Mrs. Elizabeth Fuller of Watford Place, the only daughter of Mr. John Comyne, alias Chilcott, of Tiverton in Devonshire, and of London, Merchant, who dyed ye 11th of Novb. aged 65. Silverton Chilcott, Gent, Brother of the Foundress of the School, has made an addition of £20 a year for ever."

The first master was paid £20 p.a. and his job description required him to be a model of sobriety. He was to be "...of sober and religious conversation and in communion with the Church of England."

He was to teach "40 poor boys to read, write, and cast accounts" and these boys were to "...attend dressed in new grey bonnets and grey cloth coats with broad brass buttons, tied

73. Inscription over the door to Elizabeth Fuller's Free School, opposite St Mary's churchyard.

with orange-coloured cardus ribbon...."
Some provision was made for poor girls:

"....the schoolmistress was to have £6 yearly for teaching 14 poor girls of Watford to read, knit, and work at their needle, and, if funds would permit, the girls were to be clothed with linsey-woolsey gowns of the same colour as the boys' coats, Holland bands and quives, and blue aprons.'[2]

Mrs Fuller's generosity was also directed to the poor in general and she was very specific in her instructions. Robert Clutterbuck tells us that she,

"...by her will directed, that the Treasurer should order a baker of Watford, every Saturday for ever, to deliver to the Church-wardens of Bushey for the time being, 18d. worth of wheaten bread made into 12 loaves, and to pay for the same, to be given to the poor of Bushey every Sunday after morning service, and during the service, to be placed on some convenient shelves, to be put up at the charge of her executor in Bushey Church; and after the sermon, to be carried into the Church-yard, and delivered from off her tomb-stone, to twelve poor persons of that parish, in consideration that the Churchwardens and Officers of the said parish for the time being, should keep her tombstone in good repair, and not suffer the same to be removed or disturbed."

Elizabeth Fuller died in 1709 and was buried in the Bushey churchyard of St James's. The ceremony of serving bread from her tombstone continued into the beginning of the 20th century. The tombstone is still in good repair, but

74. *The tomb of Elizabeth Fuller, in the churchyard of St James, Bushey.*

75. *The tombstone of Elizabeth Fuller's brother embedded in the wall of the Free School building, to the right of the front door.*

her coat of arms placed prominently on top of the tomb, and the inscription, are suffering from the effects of time.

Her brother was buried much closer to home, alongside the Free School near the front door. Clutterbuck, writing in 1815, tells us that "in the Church-yard, on an altar-tomb, abutting against the front of Mrs. Fuller's Charity School-house: 'Here lieth the Body of Silvester Chilcott, Gent.only Brother to Mrs.Eliz. Fuller, the Donor of this School, who dep. This Life Jan.9.1716." The altar-tomb mentioned in 1815 has gone, but the inscription remains sited under a window, and actually built in to the structure of the school.

An entry in Henry Lomas's diary for 3 April 1827 shows that the running of the school was not totally harmonious:

"Complaints having been made against Mr Hawkes master of the Watford Free School and also Parish Clerk, that he neglected the learning of the children, and the Trustees considering him incapable of performing the duties of both situations with accuracy gave him the priviledge of making choice of which he would hold singly. He chose the latter when Mr Camfil [Camfield] teacher of the Earl of Essex's national school was appointed to the free school with permission to have ten Pay scholars and an Evening School."

The charitable donations bequeathed to Fuller's school were never quite enough but in 1753 the Trustees were able to increase the annual income for the school from £52 to £250 per annum. The school closed in August 1882 with the opening of a new school building in Derby Road, called the Watford Central School, which cost £6000.[3] The continuity remained as the trustees of the Free School became Governors of the Derby Road school. This building however was not large enough for the purpose, which led to a Girls only school in Lady's Close being built in 1907.

76 & 77. *Two views of the Free School building, above in c1880, and below in 2005.*

78. *The Derby Road Watford Central School. It was opened by the Earl of Clarendon in 1883.*

79. *Pupils at the Central School, early 20th century.*

THE CREATION OF THE WATFORD GRAMMAR SCHOOLS

These schools came into being on 29 June 1882 when two secondary schools, one for boys, and one for girls, educated students initially up to the age of 16, but this was later extended to 17 years. The schools became officially known as the Watford Grammar Schools.

The first headmaster of the boys' school was a Mr. W R Carter BA who had 220 pupils. The first headmistress of the girls' school was a Miss Annie Coles with only 78 pupils. The boys' school operated with 10 assistant masters and the girls' school 9 assistant mistresses.

By the beginning of the 1880s, Henry Williams was able to comment that the changes in educational facilities between the 1830s and 1870s had been dramatic:

"forty years ago the only public schools at Watford were Mrs Fuller's Free School, one in the Rickmansworth Road, belonging to the Cassiobury estate, the Infant School in the High Street, and a small one in Butcher's Yard ... Forty boys and twenty girls was the limit at Mrs Fuller's school, about sixty at the school in the Rickmansworth Road, and about twenty at Broderick's school, making a total of about 150: while the number of children educated in our public schools at this time is 1,250."

Sir Stanley Rous (1895-1986) was a master here for thirteen years before the last war. He was to become world famous as the leading voice of English football. He was secretary of the FA from 1934 to 1961, and president of the world football body, FIFA as from 1961. It was Rous who introduced the red card / yellow card system.

In 2005 Watford Grammar School for Boys was chosen as the location for filming Alan Bennett's award-winning play, *The History Boys*. The most elegant part of the school is its red-brick Grade II main building, but much of the filming will be done in the 1970s block, which Bennett and the director Nicholas Hytner, thought ideal to portray the period of the play.

The School, which is comprehensive but permitted to admit 35% of pupils on the basis of academic ability, in 2004 came top of the *Financial Times* 1,000 league table based on A-level results.

1   Salmon, *History of Hertfordshire* (1728)
2   *Victoria County History*, Vol. 2 p96 (1902)
3   *Ibid*
4   *Sunday Telegraph*, 26 June 2005

The Poor and the Sick

THE WORKHOUSE

The early Vestry minutes illustrate that the poor were seen as a burden to be either exploited or moved on as quickly as possible. Two volumes survive covering the period 1693 to 1812. The following is an entry from 1694:

> "That in case of sickness no physic [doctor] be allowed to the poor, but in providential distress, plague, or small-pox, broken bones or wounds, and where there is occasion for blooding... that the name of all such as doe or shall receive such collections shall be registered in the book of rates of the poor, and so long as they shall receive such collection they shall wear on the right shoulder of their uppermost garment a brass badge with the letters W.P., denoting them to be Watford Poor."

By 1696 the wearing of this badge became required under Act of Parliament for the poor of all districts.

In illustration 80 note the references to 'Vagrant Beggars' being 'whippd' before being issued a pass to return to their home districts, thus avoiding Watford bearing any further expense in their upkeep. On 28 October 1689 Richard Man, a sturdy, vagrant beggar was whipped according to the law along with his wife and two small children before being issued a pass and sent back to his home parish.

In 1698 it was

> "ordered and agreed that ye overseers of the poor shall remove the poor people dwelling in the cottages under the school into some other dwellings by the 15th March for if they the overseers shall continue them any longer in ye said cottages we do likewise agree that ye overseers of the parish shall pay yearly and every year to the church wardens and their successors the sum of £3 yearly for the use of the parish church."

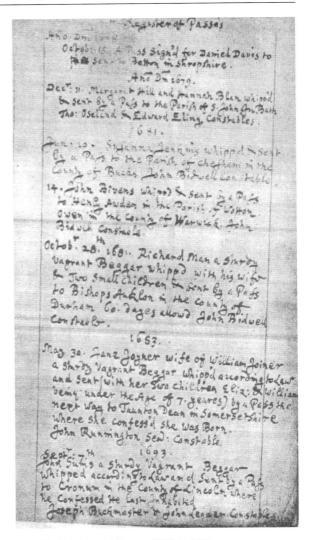

80. *The Register of Passes 1679 to 1693.*

As for poor children, in 1699 it was decided that they "with all convenient speed [be] bound out apprentices by ye church wardens and overseers and that they make a double rate for the cloathing and putting them out accordingly."

Once Parliament had passed an Act enabling parishes to provide workhouses, Watford in 1721 decided to open one. This was built in Church Street overlooking the churchyard, and cost about £158. By 1740 the inmates were obliged to "pick stones for the repairing of the

81. The former Watford Workhouse, now the Schrodells Wing of Watford General Hospital in Vicarage Road. It is Grade II listed.

highways". However, two years later, a petition signed by 57 residents asked for the workhouse to be pulled down and the poor to get their aid as before, in hovels outside. The petition was not approved. The petitioners were probably displeased that year that "several poor persons have made complaint that their weekly allowance is not sufficient and are dissatisfied therewith. It is ordered that those dissatisfied … shall be provided for by the overseers."

A record from 1769 sums up the attitude to the poor, stating that they "are to be properly employed and confined from running about the town and parish in the manner they have done, which has been much complained of."[1] The poor could also be exploited to the benefit of the parish. In the numerous silk mills and other factories employers were allowed to bid for the labour of anyone aged between 6 and 60. Where no such work was available, the poor were set to digging gravel for the roads. Their pay went straight to the Overseer at the workhouse.

The workhouse itself was run under an early form of public-private initiative. The contractor undertook to feed the workhouse inhabitants for a fixed sum. In 1754 this was £370 and in 1798, probably due to the increase in the number of poor, £1,175. The inhabitants were fed on a diet of "course flour, pease whole and split, oatmeal, salt butter, cheese, beef… and sugar". It is unlikely that the contractors distributed all the food they were being paid for. The records describe the Church Street workhouse as filthy, the occupants in a perpetual state of starvation and, during the winter, cold. The fireplaces are described as insufficient to warm the rooms. Disease was prevalent, especially smallpox. Those inmates that succumbed were shifted to the 'pesthouse', a primitive form of isolation hospital, which stood in what is now Willow Lane. This was hardly conducive to recovery for in 1754 the pesthouse was described as not being fit to receive sick persons.

'An Account of Several Workhouses' in 1725

refers to Watford Workhouse, and again in 1777 a parliamentary report mentions it, with up to 100 inmates in the Church Street building. The Poor Law Amendment Act of 1834 amongst other things brought in Poor Law Unions, in which parishes were obliged to combine so as to build larger workhouses to achieve an economy brought about by scale. A Watford Union workhouse was built in 1836-7 on the south side of Hagden Lane. The site of the old workhouse in Church Street was sold and converted into a shop and cottages. The new building was renamed Shrodells in the 1930s, and later became a geriatric hospital. When Watford General Hospital was developed on this site, this central block was used as offices.

Records of the number of inmates at the Union workhouse and the volumes of food and drink survive.

"The average cost per head of indoor paupers for the year ending Lady Day, 1883, for food, clothing, and burials was 3s. 7d. per week:-

Inmates in the house at Lady Day, 1883	*237*
Number of persons relieved in the workhouse for the Year ended Lady Day, 1883	*642*
Out of the workhouse	*2331*
Vagrants and tramps relieved at the workhouse	*6595*
Paupers receiving relief 1st January, 1883	*1130*

The out-relief for Watford [that is aid to the poor outside the confines of the workhouse] in the year 1882 amounted to £1,543 8s. 1¼d. and for the year 1883 to £1,564 12s 9½d. The total amount levied for the year 1883, in Watford parish, was 2s. 6d. in the pound. Contributions from poor rates for poor law expenditure, 9d. in the pound; ditto for county rates, 2¼d. in the pound; ditto for police, 2¾d. in the pound; and ditto for Lunatic Asylum rates, 1½d. in the pound."[2]

The burial of workhouse residents was put out to tender and carefully regulated. The tender specified that costs were to include coffins, shrouds, caps, payments to bearers to the church

and all burial fees and other expenses.

"Only three sizes of coffin were to be used – for adults, children over 12 years, and children under 12 years. The coffins were to be made of good sound elm one inch thick, properly pitched inside; the elm boards should be considered the trade inch to allow for the cutting of the saw. Shrouds and caps were to be made of calico, samples required. The contractors for the burial of paupers should provide a cloth-pall for adults and a sheet for children at their funerals."

At a meeting in November 1835 it was decided that "...no additional ornaments were to be added to coffins, and that any extra expense incurred on the burial of paupers was to be paid for by relatives or friends of the deceased. The cost of funerals varied quite considerably ranging from £1. 2s. 0d. to £1. 6s.[3]

A Watford resident looking back to the 1850s remembers that:

"In the Watford Field Road, formerly called Farthing Lane, stand the People's Hall and Ragged Schools, supported by the Dissenters of the town, who are doing good work among the children of the lower classes. On Christmas Day of each year a large number of Children are entertained to a good dinner in the hall, and a number of poor adults have dinners given them to take home. This is done by subscription, and many of the subscribers wait on the little ones at their annual feast. In the early part of the present century this hall was the Wesleyan Chapel...'[4]

HOSPITALS

Watford was served by the Victoria Cottage Hospital, built in 1885 and situated in Vicarage Road. After the First World War, and with Watford's rapidly increasing population, this became inadequate and a new hospital was built in Rickmansworth Road, and named the Peace Memorial Hospital. It was opened by Princess Mary in 1925.

This too was outgrown and the Watford General Hospital was opened in Vicarage Road on the site, as we have seen above, of the old workhouse.

82. The Peace Memorial Hospital opened by Princess Mary in 1925.

In consequence of the very great prevalence of small-pox in the town of Watford, which was considered to be mainly attributable to parents and others having the charge of children labouring under the complaint suffering them to appear in public, the board of guardians have issued an order and notice, that parents or any persons having the care of children labouring under the complaint, who shall permit them to appear in public or go abroad, will be indicted and punished according to law. Within the last fortnight the disease appears to have greatly extended itself in the neighbourhood.—*Evening paper.*

83. Extract from The Times, *31 October, 1838.*

ALMSHOUSES

Chauncy, writing at the end of the 17th century, said:

"The Family of the *Morisons* have also erected eight Alms-houses for eight poor Widows in Watford, made a handsome Yard before and Gardens behind the Houses, and for their Maintenance given each of them two Shillings a Week, two hundred of Faggots, Cloath sufficient to make them a Gown and new Hats every Year, which the said Earl of Essex, the lineal descendent of that Family, doth constantly pay and allow."[5]

They were built by Francis, 2nd Earl of Bed-

ford to house eight poor women from Watford, Chenies and Langley. In 1771 plans were made for a new road to the almshouses, which determine the line of the road today. In 1930 there was concern over the fate of the almshouses and the eight old ladies who occupied them, due to the possible purchase of the site for a car park. The first Council proposal to purchase and preserve the almshouses was lost by two votes, but subsequent amendments from the Highways Committee were adopted and the almshouses survived. The Mayor later appealed for funds to repair and preserve them. £100 was donated by the Watford Corporation, and an additional £400 came from other sources.[6]

THE SALTERS' COMPANY

A local traveller and author who writes under the name of 'An Old Inhabitant' observed that "near St Andrew's Church, are the Almshouses of the Salters' Company, which will accommodate twelve women and six men; they were erected in 1864, and the area of the ground is 5 acres." These almshouses were the replacement for the almshouses founded by Sir

84. The Bedford and Essex Almshouses, now nos. 1-8 Church Street, viewed from St Mary's churchyard. These are the oldest inhabited buildings in Watford.

85. The gates to the Salters' Almshouses in Church Road, dating from 1887.

86. *Salters' Almshouses in Church Road.*

88. *The London Orphan Asylum in Orphanage Road, built in 1871. It is now converted to private dwellings.*

87. *The former chapel of the London Orphan Asylum.*

LONDON ORPHAN ASYLUM.—The 68th anniversary festival in aid of the funds of this institution took place last night at Willis's Rooms. Baron Henry de Worms, M.P., presided, and among those present were the Sheriffs of London and Middlesex, Mr. Alderman Fowler, M.P., and Mr. H. J. Waterlow, Baron George de Worms, Mr. A. R. Capel (treasurer of the institution), Mr. A. Hanbury, Mr. John Kemp-Welch, Mr. E. J. Layton, Mr. Seager Hunt, and Mr. W. Rivington. The chairman, in giving the toast of " Prosperity to the Institution," traced its progress since the year 1813, when it was founded by Dr. Andrew Reed. In 1822 there were 156 children within the walls, supported at a cost of £4,357 by 4,608 subscribers. In 1880 the number had risen to 542 children ; there were 9,150 subscribers, and the income was £17,000. The benefits of the charity had been enjoyed by 4,450 orphan children, and there were now about 550 children in the asylum. One great feature of the institution was that its advantages were not limited to any one class, while the scale of education was very high, qualifying the boys and girls to pass the Oxford Local Examinations, and the examinations of the Science and Art Department. Having very little property—nine-tenths of the income being derived from donations and subscriptions—the managers had been obliged last year to expend a large bequest of £4,000 in order to meet current expenses. Describing the scene he had recently witnessed in the institution at Watford, the chairman made an earnest appeal for support. Donations and subscriptions to the amount of £3,700 were announced.

89. A report on a fund-raising dinner for the Orphanage, reported in The Times *10 March 1881.*

Nicholas Ambrose in 1578 for the Salters' Company in Monkwell Street, London. When the land was needed for warehouses the new almshouses were erected just outside Watford in 1864.[7] They can still be seen in Church Road.

THE ORPHANAGE

The London Orphanage Asylum was the successor to one built in Clapton, east London in 1813. It was decided that the children deserved a more salubrious location and Watford's railway, easy accessibility and its reputation as a healthy town in a healthy county led to a new asylum being built in the vicinity of Watford Junction railway station. The foundation stone was laid by the then Prince of Wales in 1869, and the building was opened in 1872 by Princess Mary of Cambridge. The foundation that ran the orphanage was specifically instructed to "maintain, clothe, and educate respectable fatherless children of either sex, who are without means adequate to their support, wherever resident." The children were admitted between the ages of 6 and 11 and had to leave on reaching 15 years.

The buildings still stand in Orphanage Road, and have been converted to private dwellings.

1   Vestry record quoted by Saunders
2   Williams p117
3   Norris, Phyllis, *The Beginnings of the Watford Union Workhouse* (1987)
4   Williams p117
5   Williams p81
6   Chauncy p364
7   Information Watford Council
8   Harben, Henry H, *A Dictionary of London* (1918)

More Churches

HOLY ROOD – ONE OF THE FINEST CHURCHES IN ENGLAND

Holy Rood is one of the two Grade I listed buildings in Watford. It was built to serve the increasing number of Catholics in Watford during the second half of the 19th century. In 1861 a young priest, Fr. Bampfield, came to Watford looking for a suitable place to say Mass. He found only four or five Catholic families, poor and living in miserable habitations quite unsuitable for a Mass centre. He inserted notices in the papers for Catholics to come forward and by 1863 he was able to hire a room in Carey Place, which joined the High Street near to no. 137, a small thoroughfare that no longer exists. About sixty people attended, including a number of agricultural workers from Ireland.

Bampfield was determined to establish a church and his first building was a wooden hut in Upper Paddock Road near Bushey railway arches. He then found a site in Water Lane near the High Street where he built a chapel, which was in use until Holy Rood was opened in 1890. Holy Rood remains today very close to what its architect, John Francis Bentley, meant it to be. Sir Nikolaus Pevsner, author of the *Buildings of England* series, calls it "One of the noblest examples of the refined, knowledgeable and sensitive Gothic Revival of that time." The architectural writer, H S Goodhart-Rendell, thought that it had a strong claim to be considered the most lovely church that the 19th century gave to England.

ST ANDREW'S

Watford's continued growth meant that new churches of all denominations were required.

90. Holy Rood church, one of Watford's two Grade I listed buildings.

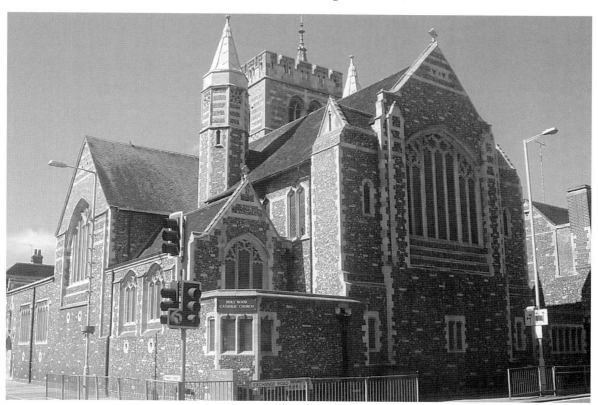

91. The restored Rood Loft of Holy Rood church.

St Andrew's in Church Road was the first new Anglican church. Begun in 1853 it was completed in 1857 to designs by S S Teulon. It lies off the Hempstead Road in the direction of

92. St Andrew's in Church Road, completed in 1857.

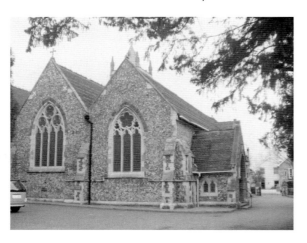

Leavesden, occupying land donated by the then Earl of Essex. It was at that time noted for having "modern ventilation" and being lit by gaslight. Much of the original furniture was made or donated by members of the church and the beautiful stained glass windows date from around 1865.

ST JOHN'S

In 1871 St Mary's underwent a major restoration which meant erecting a temporary iron building in which to conduct services. On completion the temporary church was moved to a site in what is now Sutton Road, and this later became the parish church of St John the Apostle and Evangelist. The current building was dedicated in 1893.

BEECHEN GROVE BAPTIST CHURCH

Baptist worship is first noted in Watford when in 1669 we read of 'ye house of JNO Crawley, a joiner, Watford – Anabaptists." In 1707 the Baptists formed a church, and in 1721 erected a Meeting House (in what became Meeting House Alley). In 1877 the Beechen Grove church in Clarendon Road was opened, unusually in 'later Romanesque' style. It was built on land adjoining an early Baptist burial ground containing graves made between 1721 and 1861. These were removed in 1963 to make way for a car park.

THE WESLEYANS

Methodism in Watford dates from 1808 when they had a place of worship in Hedge Yard. There then followed a number of moves as the community increased, which included a site in Water Lane, then Farthing Lane, and finally in Queens Road.

Crime and Punishment

HIGHWAYMEN

Watford, lying at the conjunction of several major roads, provided a copious number of victims, followed by a ready means of escape, for highwaymen. Hardly a town is without a Dick Turpin legend, but it is believed that Dick Turpin did indeed lodge and take refreshment on more than one occasion at the Green Man. An early nineteenth-century resident of Watford writes that,

"at one time there was a dell on the left hand side of the road at Crook Log, and a footpath along the bank through the underwood and trees, but it was enclosed by the late General Walker. In the seclusion of that footpath, Richard [Turpin] when a footpad, eased a traveller coming into Watford of a large sum of money, leaving him nearly dead in the dell, the robber having inflicted a severe punishment on him for endeavouring to save his well-filled purse."

The same inhabitant goes on to comment that many less exalted robbers operated in and around Watford. Hamper Mill Lane, Hempstead, St Albans and Rickmansworth roads were their favourite haunts. He complains that many were a lot more violent than Turpin,

"It is said that in Hamper Mill Lane one man [victim] was killed on the spot, and after being robbed of everything of value he had on him, was dragged into the wood, where he laid for many days....'[1]

From an article in *The Times* of 3 August 1807:

"A Gentleman, on Sunday night, returning to town from Watford, on horse back was stopped in one of the lanes between Edgware and Hendon, and robbed by a single highwayman, armed with pistols, who took from him his watch, and about fifteen shillings, and rode off. On Wednesday, a parcel was left for the party robbed, at his place of abode, containing the watch and a pound note, with this singular line,

written in a female hand: "I restore your property, as I now don't want it.—Farewell."

THE WATFORD STOCKS

Watford's stocks stood under the old market-house, and were probably taken down during the early part of the 19th century. Offenders, typically poachers, wife-beaters and drunks, were placed in the stocks and were pelted with rotten eggs, mud, stones and water.

Henry Williams tells us of an incident early in the 19th century:

"A man named Billy Lovett, who resided at the Rookery, was put into the stocks three different times for cruelty to his children. He suffered them to remain so long unwashed that it required considerable force to remove the dirt, when he used a scrubbing-brush to cleanse their skin, applying so much force that he not only removed the dirt, but the skin also."

Until the early 1800s the 'cage' or lock-up stood near St Mary's. It has been described as having an uninviting appearance, strongly built with an abundance of bars, bolts and locks, with a small square hole in the door to allow light and air, conversation and the passing through of food and drink. An early Watford resident commented that the confinement was not the worst of the miscreant's problems:

"The boys of the day were a precocious set of imps, and took delight in pelting with mud and filth offenders against the laws of the land; and it often happened that when some imprisoned man was gazing listlessly on the outer world through the bars of his prison, a lump of mud, thrown in his face, would cause him to recede to the back of his dark and loathsome dungeon, there to curse his assailant, and remove the filth from his face with the tail of his coat or the back of his hand."[2]

More serious punishments are recorded in the Hertfordshire Sessions Rolls:

"Jno. Butler of Watford convicted of stealing two horseshoes and 7 pieces of horseshoes from James Darvell, Blacksmith. Ordered to be whipped at the Market Post, Watford, till his body be bloody and then discharged on paying his fees."

93. *The former Watford County Court in Kings Close, built c.1858. Photo 2005.*

"Thos. Humphries convicted of stealing a silver spoon from the house of Joshua Pickersgill, of Watford. Transported for 7 years."[3]

JUSTICE

The Sikh Community Centre in Kings Close occupies what was the Watford County Court, built *c*.1858. The old cells are now in the side entrance block facing Kings Close, and the jurors' room was at the front on the first floor.

Before the Court was built the magistrates held their sittings at the Essex Arms each Tuesday. An early 19th-century report describes the court "in a room now the lobby of the Corn Exchange. A rude railing about 3 feet high kept the people at a proper distance from the magistrates' table which was a very ordinary piece of furniture covered with green baize, and the chairs on which the justices sat had wooden seats and were without cushions."

The lists of Watford magistrates of 1871 and 1891[4] show them, unsurprisingly, to be the local great and good. In 1871 there was Lord Malden, Lt Col. Foskett, the Earl of Essex, the Hon. R Capel, R R Carew and Major Foskett. Twenty years later Capel and Carew are still there, accompanied by J S Gilliat MP, Sir James Longden and the Hon. A Holland-Hibbert, a son of Viscount Knutsford. Many of them were local landowners who dealt harshly with poachers, as indeed did magistrates all over the country. As late as 1892 a coachman from Watford was fined £3 with 10s costs for going equipped to poach. Failure to pay would have led to one month's hard labour.

A 1790 report in *The Times* commended the Hertfordshire magistrates "for their vigilance in suppressing every attempt to introduce prize fighting in that County. A battle was to have been fought at Otterspool in Hertfordshire on Monday last, but through the vigilance of that very active Magistrate, Mr Clutterbuck of Watford, it was prevented, and ring-leaders of the mob are bound over to appear at the next Quarter-Sessions. However, the following year The Times announced that

"The people of WATFORD may now, with FALSTAFF, 'take any man's horses' – for the death of MR CLUTTERBUCK has left the town without a Magistrate."

EARLY TRAFFIC OFFENCES

The court records of the years 1871 and 1891 contain a number of early traffic offences. John Graham, a haycart driver of Few Onions Farm in Bovingdon, was fined 2/6d with 6 shillings costs or seven days hard labour for riding while asleep in his hay cart in Watford. George Brown, a beerhouse keeper of "Bushey Heth", was fined forty shillings with 13/6d costs or two months in prison for the "furious driving of his horse and cart in the High Street, Watford." And William Bryant of Bushey was fined one shilling with 15/6d costs or fourteen days in prison for leaving a horse and cart unattended in Watford.

More unusually, James Marshall, a butcher from Ruislip, was fined 2 shillings plus costs for driving a cart in Watford which did not bear the owner's name. He told the magistrates that he had "used it in the same condition for twenty-five years".

A FAMOUS MURDER

It was the Watford magistrates, Robert Clutterbuck and John Finch Mason who carried out the investigations and interrogations in a case variously referred to as the 'Weare' or 'Elstree' murder. This occurred on 24 October 1823. The accused were John Thurtell and Joseph Hunt, charged with the murder of William Weare on account of an unpaid gambling debt.

The murder took place in Gills Hill Lane in Radlett, about three miles from Watford. Thurtell, born in 1794, was the son of the mayor of Norwich. Coming from a well-to-do family, he was a wealthy gambler. This was an unusual crime and the newspapers were very interested in the detail. Several thousand books were sold immediately after the trial, relating Thurtell's demeanour during his last hours before his public hanging at Hertford Gaol – there were 15,000 spectators.

The murder occurred outside the Wagon and

Horses Inn, Watling Street on the Elstree-Radlett road. The inn is still there. Thurtell drew his pistol and fired at Weare's face. The shot glanced off Weare's cheekbone and then Thurtell attacked his victim with a penknife, cutting his throat and, just to make absolutely sure, forced the barrel of the pistol into Weare's skull. Thurtell asked two friends, William Probert and a local man, Joseph Hunt, to help him dispose of the body. Initially the corpse lay buried in the garden of Probert's cottage in Gills Hill, but when darkness came they decided to move it to a pond in Elstree, at a point called Hill Slough where Watling Street and Allum Lane meet.

However, the murder had been witnessed and Clutterbuck and Finch Mason undertook the investigation while being based at the Essex Arms in Watford High Street. Thurtell and Hunt were conveyed "in separate chaises" to Watford and were "kept strictly watched in separate rooms at the Essex Arms Inn, where the investigation before the Magistrates commenced at half-past ten o'clock at night.[5]

Hunt turned King's Evidence and led the authorities to the body, which was then recovered and taken to the Artichoke public house in Watling Street. The surgeon who examined the body was a Watford man, Thomas Abel Ward, and it was a medical person, Pidcock of Watford, who declared that the pistol used in the murder had fragments on the barrel which were a "portion of the brains of a human being."

THE LAST WOMAN TO BE HANGED IN HERTFORDSHIRE

Another murder that received dramatic coverage and caused much controversy was the killing by poison in 1899 of Caroline Ansell at the Leavesden Asylum for 'London imbeciles'. Ansell, an inmate, received parcels of foodstuff in the post, which she ate. A few days later she died of poisoning and a post mortem was held under the auspices of the Watford coroner. The police later arrested Caroline's sister Mary Ansell who, it was discovered, had insured her sister's life for £11 5s should Caroline die a natural death after 6 March 1899. At her trial in June, Mary Ansell pleaded not guilty but

EXECUTION OF MARY ANN ANSELL.

Mary Ann Ansell, 18, domestic servant, was executed in St. Albans Gaol yesterday morning for the wilful murder of her sister, Caroline Ansell, aged 26, an inmate of Leavesden Asylum, Watford, by means of poisoned cake conveyed to the deceased through the post.

The police-court missioner stated yesterday to a Press representative that he had opportunities of conversation with Mary Ansell before the death sentence was passed, and though reluctant to speak he said, at length, "I do not think she was insane. In all my dealings with her I have come to the conclusion that her demeanour was more sullen than anything else. I have seen the parents, and the father emphatically denies that there is insanity in the family." As to the murdered sister Caroline, the father said to the missioner, according to the latter's statement, "she was as right as you are until her brother was killed, and she then fretted so much that her mind gave way."

The inquest on the body of Mary Ansell was held at 10 o'clock within the gaol. The chief warder having given the usual formal testimony, the Coroner observed, "I suppose everything was carried out in a satisfactory manner?" to which the witness replied, "Yes, it was." A juryman.—"Was death instantaneous?" Witness.—"It was. There was not a movement of any kind." After the medical evidence the Coroner summed up, and the jury returned the customary verdict in such cases.

94. *From* The Times, 20 July 1899.

was not believed by the jury and she was sentenced to hang at St Albans in July. The *Daily Mail* launched a vigorous campaign to save her on the grounds of presumed insanity and tried to prove that this ran in the Ansell family. The newspaper received 10,000 letters of support. There was a general expectancy that she would be reprieved and the day before the execution 100 Members of Parliament signed a petition to allow at the very least a temporary postponement. The Home Secretary rejected this on the grounds that the prison service believed her to be sane. 2000 people gathered outside St Albans Gaol on the morning of the execution. Mary Ansell's body was buried in the prison grounds.[6]

KEEPING ORDER

Prior to the founding of the Hertfordshire Constabulary in 1841, policing was based on the headborough and constable system, officers elected by the manorial courts or by the vestry. This system, we are told by William Lambard in 1614, was designed to include the "suppression of drunkenness, popish recusants, [and to] deal with rogues and beggars whilst checking weights and measures."[7] A vestry minute of 1697 tells us that "it is ordered that Richard Flood being Headborough for the hamlet of Cashio (and John Buckmaster the constable dying with the year) serving the office of constable in the room of the said John Buckmaster and the said Richard Flood, being a poor labouring man, that £1 be allowed him and above his bill as it is now agreed unto by this vestry, so that in the whole he is to be allowed £1. 4s out of the Constable's rate."

A resident, born in Watford in 1828 and writing in 1883, recalls that two watchmen protected the inhabitants of the town from two guard boxes in the High Street, one situated near the pond and the other at the far end. They would 'call the hours' through the night commencing with 'Past eleven'.

"On one occasion somebody played a practical joke on the watchman. Having cried the hour of 'One', he retired to his box and fell into an uneasy slumber, snoring loudly, which attracted the attention of a passer-by who had been turned out of the Horns public house, considerably the worse for drink. He went behind the box, put his shoulder to it, and, with one mighty push, overturned it, and made the occupant a prisoner. When the watchman recovered from the fright caused by the suddenness with which his equilibrium had been disturbed, and found himself a prisoner (for his box had fallen over with the door downwards), he shouted lustily for help, but for some time failed to do more than make the neighbouring dogs bark; at last his cries were heard by the people residing near, who went to his help, and on releasing him found him much exhausted, and considerably bruised about the head and face."[8]

Another resident, described as 'old' when he wrote his recollections in 1916, says that the first police station

"was a private house, now number 193 High Street, and the force consisted of one Superintendent Captain Kelly and one constable, who used to be called 'Ducky' as he wore white-trousers. A watchman patrolled the High Street at night and called out the time and state of the weather. He had a watch box, which stood on the grass, near Little Elms."

95. *The Robert Peel pub in King Street, which once housed Watford's first police station.*

The description probably applies to the 1840s.

Another recollection from an old resident, recalling probably the same period, relates that "My father was one of the two constables or watchmen in the days before policemen. He carried a lantern and truncheon and walked the High Street, calling out the hours of the night. He was Town Crier too, and charged a shilling for 'crying' anything lost."[9]

The site of Watford's first police station is on the corner of King Street and High Street, and is the appropriately named 'Robert Peel' public house, which bears the date 1888 on the side wall.

LACK OF BOBBIES ON THE BEAT

The modern complaint of the lack of policemen on the beat is not new. A report from 1849 tells us that "an inspector and two men reside in the town and attend to the district. They belong to the county police. This force, or that share of its attention that falls to the town, seems to be insufficient for its protection, since some few of the inhabitants contribute as much as 2 shillings annually as a voluntary rate for private watching."[10]

TELEPHONES AND BICYCLES

1891 saw the arrival of telephones for the Hertfordshire police service. The Watford force received its own telephone connecting it to Bushey, Rickmansworth, St Albans, Hatfield and the Clerk of the Peace in 1893. Whereas before it had been possible for the duty policeman to sleep through the night, this was about to change. At nights, the telephone was switched through to the bedroom of the office.

An experimental bicycle was purchased for the Watford station in 1893. In 1895 when the number of bikes reached 11, the Hertford constabulary requested that the "names and numbers of officers of all ranks competent to ride bicycles are to be sent into this office, and names of officers are to be sent in as they learn to ride a machine." Danger money of 3d per hour was payable to constables prepared to ride the machines. The force received its first motor car in October 1905.

1   Williams p192
2   *Ibid* p195
3   Saunders p37
4   V A Ingram, 'Crime and Punishment in Watford, 1871 and 1891' in *Aspects of Nineteenth Century Watford*, p71 (Watford WEA 1987)
5   *A Complete History and Development of All the Extraordinary Circumstances and Events Connected with the Murder of Mr. Weare: Together with the Trial at Large: Including the Speeches of Counsel-Examination of Evidence-Defence. The Whole forming a Genuine Series of Gambling Biography.* (1824).
6   Connell, Nicholas, and Stratton, Ruth, *Hertfordshire Murders* (2003)
7   Osborn, Neil, *The Story of Hertfordshire Police*, published by Hertfordshire Countryside, 1969
8   Williams p193
9   Saunders quoting from the recollections of Mr H West, for many years Watford's Town Crier

In Transition

In truth, Watford retained its rural nature right into the first decades of the 20th century. As late as the 1850s people who lived in the none too salubrious courts off the High Street kept poultry which scratched around during the day in the High Street. There was a cattle pound in St Albans Road for the detention of animals that had become lost. Cattle and corn were still sold in the market place. A memoir tells us that in the middle of the 19th century "most houses had pig-sties in the back garden..." and that "women and children after harvest, went into the field... gathering up what corn was left..." The reality would have been a bustling High Street that smelled of livestock, horses and industrial effluent.

The then local authority, the Vestry, could not cope with the increased population, for its principal officers, including churchwardens and highway surveyors, were unpaid. It was incapable even of dealing with the frequent flooding of the town. Henry Hunter in *The History of London* (1811) noted that the town "consists of one very long street, which is extremely dirty during the winter, and the waters of the river at the entrance of the town are often so much swelled by the floods as to be impassable."

By the 1840s conditions had deteriorated rapidly especially in the matter of drainage. A letter dated 26 August 1849 from the Medical Officer of the Watford Poor Law Union to the Watford Board of Guardians commented:

"Not only are the courts and alleys in this pestiferous state, but the high street also, where all sorts of most offensive effluvia are met with, for to the disgrace of Watford it may be said that in addition to vegetable and animal matter floating in the open drain may constantly be detected *human dejecta* emptied from pails, tubs, etc. etc. from different houses and also swept from some of the courts into the open sewer and left to chance to be washed or cleansed away."

DISEASE

In 1848 a major cholera outbreak swept Europe, which led to Parliament passing a number of Public Health Acts. A public fear of cholera, a disease which had recently affected Abbot's Langley and Rickmansworth, as well as causing deaths in Watford itself, meant that the situation locally could not be allowed to continue. In December 1848 Watford residents petitioned the General Board of Health in London and this led to an inspection of the town between 26 and 28 February of 1849.

The meetings of the General Board were held at the Rose & Crown inn. Its Report dispels a nostalgic image of a locality still in a rural stage and governed by a benign wealthy class. In many ways instead it was beset by many of the evils in London made more public by Dickens.

The Report of 1849 tells us:

"Watford is composed of a principal street, about 1½ mile long, built along a sort of ridge sloping southwards to the river. On either side, or communicating with this street, are numerous courts and alleys, composed of small tenements, in which the bulk of the population is lodged. There are scarcely any cross streets, and the town is nowhere above 440 yards, and seldom above 200 yards broad...

Persons ignorant of road-making are appointed surveyors of highways, and there is fostered a strong party spirit fatal to all improvement."

The Report gives the population of 1831 as 5,293 and in 1841 as 5,989. Note that the effect of the railway was at this stage barely noticeable. It also quoted an 1838 description of the conditions to be found there:

"The most unhealthy localities in the town are found to be Meeting-alley, Dyson's [now Ballard's] buildings, Red Lion, Chequers, and Old-yards. The confined position of the former, and the open drains and deposit of ordure in the latter, at once account for this unhealthy condition. Few dwellings in these yards have escaped the visitation of disease, and but few of the inhabitants of them can be said ever to enjoy robust health. Those yards, which have blind extremities, such as Dyson's, are in the worst condition; having no thoroughfares, little publicity is given to the habits of the cottagers, and thus a principal stimulus to cleanliness is wanting."

The report continues:

"This was in 1838, and it will be seen that the 10 or 11 years which have elapsed have produced no improvement, nor indeed, under the existing system of government by vestry officers, is any likely to be produced."

The next section of the Report makes it clear that the sewerage arrangements were poor:

"Commencing at the top of the town, the houses below the Dog public-house have privies with open cesspools, pigsties, dung-heaps, and are without drains. The house slops are for the most part thrown into the main road and public footway, which, at the time of my visit, was in a state very offensive to passers by. This is a fever locality.

Proceeding down the street on the west side is Wells-yard, a fever locality with an overflowing cesspool, the filth from which passes down the court into another cesspool... In Stones-yard, a slaughter-house and divers nuisances open upon a public footpath. Around the Market-place, the oldest part of the town, the nuisances are very numerous... Ballard's-buildings, otherwise in a creditable state, has a very narrow passage on its south side, blocked with privies, open cesspools, and night soil [excrement], upon an unpaved surface. On the north side of the churchyard, a block of poor houses is closely shut up between the churchyard and the narrow street, with no back yard or privies whatever. Close by, against the churchyard wall, is a heap upon which the refuse of these houses is thrown. Clarke's-buildings, Crown-yard, Farthing-lane, Swan-alley, all leading from the main street into Watford Common-field, are without drainage save a few open gutters, and have all open cesspools and ill-conditioned privies."

The village pond, the subject of numerous Edwardian scenic postcards is described somewhat differently from what we see in pictures barely 50 years later,

"In the main street, opposite to one of the best houses in the town [probably Monmouth House] is a pond, dry in summer, and which when cleaned out, as is the case annually, is a very great nuisance. This pond should be filled up."

And further:

"Since this Report was drawn up the following extract from the district medical-relief book has been transmitted to me:- 'There have been four cases of fever at Brown's, in the Red Lion-yard, and two have died. The drainage is most defective, and cannot be otherwise than extremely prejudicial to the health of the inhabitants residing in the cottages in the neighbourhood. – THOS. A. WARD.'"

WATER SUPPLY

The report also mentions the water supply available in Watford.

"Water Supply. – Watford is supplied with water chiefly from wells worked with buckets... There is a public well in the main street fitted with Braithwaite's pump... Besides these waters, which are much too hard to be used for washing, rain water is largely collected from the roofs, and stored in butts and tanks or pans. It appears that the rain water storage of a cottage lasts from one to three weeks."

Because of the poor access to fresh water at that time, personal cleanliness was a problem. Residents either washed in the Colne, using a mixture of soap and sod, or in the pond at the top end of the High Street. It was hardly satisfactory: "... the water of the Upper Pond, though dirty ... is used by the neighbours for washing. This pond, above the town, and the river below it, are the only resources in case of fire."

Even the use of the Colne was partly threatened during the first part of the 19th century, when a number of attempts were made to divert its waters to supply London. Strong local interests always intervened to prevent what was seen as activity likely to be detrimental to Watford. A letter designed to prevent this damage was sent in 1840 to Sir John Sebright by the Rev. J C Clutterbuck. He believed that the springs around Watford would suffer badly, and that local interests, by which he probably meant brewing in particular, would suffer. The following figures included in his letter emphasise how even at this early date, Watford was growing industrially:

Local Board of Health pumping 500,000 gallons daily

The Railway Company 250,000 gallons daily

Colne Valley Water Company pumping 270,000 gallons daily

Total daily usage: 1,020,000 gallons daily

In 1852 a company named The London (Watford) Spring Water Company observed that the waters of Watford were of an "admirable quality" being "utterly free from all organic or putrescible animal or vegetable matter." They planned to supply London by means of "constantly charged" pipes "without the intervention of a cistern" and would thus, courtesy of Watford, supply London with water which was free "from animal and vegetable matter" and was soft, fresh, bright, agreeable, and uniform in temperature. The company concluded that Watford's water had "every quality that is desirable in a water for the domestic uses of the population of a large metropolis."

SLUM LANDLORDS

Throughout the latter half of the 19th century and into the first thirty years of the 20th century parts of Watford suffered appalling housing conditions. Dwellings without any form of sanitation or amenities had been built after the arrival of the railway, partly to house the navvies who worked on the railway, and partly to house those workers coming into Watford in the wake of the rapid industrialisation of the town.

A report from the middle of the 19th century chastises the slum landlords:

"Those who are most largely interested in cottage property of the worst description, and who are enabled by the imperfection of the existing law, to take advantage of the poverty of their tenants, to escape poor's rates, and who do not possess foresight sufficient to see that

96. *Chapman's Yard 1893, situated almost opposite where now stands Watford Museum.*

economical sanitary reforms will augment the value of their property, are precisely the class of persons who are generally opposed to any attempt to better the condition of the poor. With them, or among them, are others who have an interest in keeping up the present high price of gas, which can be done by influence in vestry."

GAS SUPPLY

Watford was supplied with gas by means of a monopoly private company and by 1849 there were 55 street lamps which were lit for eight and a half months of the year. The town paid the provider 4 shillings per lamp. An inhabitant wrote that "...the tax laid upon the town by the bad management of its surveyors of highways, and the determination of the Gas Company to keep up their prices, is very severe, and would be materially lightened under a proper system of management." The complainant continues with a call for competition: "....the town should possess a power of pur-

97. *Church Street in October 1892, cited in the mid 19th century as an example of the appalling conditions. However, these buildings were not demolished until 1893.*

chasing the works, or of establishing others, and letting them by contract."

FIGHTING FIRES

As Watford industrialised, the number of reported fires increased. The closeness of the buildings, the nature of the building materials led to a number of disasters. The lack of an established fire brigade, and the voluntary nature of fire fighting meant that often it was difficult to contain these fires.

John Baldwin, a rat catcher, was sentenced to death in 1834 for setting fire to a Watford farm. He was hanged at Hertford and buried in St Mary's churchyard near the south wall of the church *(see ill. 99)*.

A short while later another fire occurred in Beechen Grove at a silk mill. Tragically, several horses in nearby stables were burnt to death because, terrified by the fire, they refused to come out of their stable stalls. In 1853 the old Market House in Market Place burnt down. A contemporary report noted that

"Shortly after the fire was discovered the parish engine was brought round, and plenty of willing hands being present, it was speedily set to work, and water thrown on the burning building. Due to the lack of water and the fire spreading rapidly ... the old pump which stood close to the Market House was brought into use... a number of men and lads were called together and placed at intervals from the Market House to a pump in the Essex Arms Hotel-yard, from which water was supplied and handed from one to the other in the parish leather buckets and several pails lent by the inhabitants, and the engine thereby kept at work."

The Market House, where corn was stored, could not be saved.

After a fire in 1867 at Brightwell's Farm it was decided that the existing methods were so inefficient and ineffective that a fire brigade for Watford should be formed. The Watford and Bushey Volunteer Fire Brigade was duly set up. The volunteers paid for their own uniforms at a cost of £5 per man. Another major fire in the High Street in December 1872, at which the brigade brought three of their engines to bear did a large amount of damage, destroying the Masonic Hall and the roof of the Corn Exchange. The saving of the Essex Arms was regarded as a major success for the newly formed brigade.

Eventually the High Street fire station proved inadequate and in February 1961 the station moved to the corner of Rickmansworth Road and Whippendell Road.

CROWN COURT.—(*Before Mr. Justice* LITTLEDALE.)
John Baldwin, a labourer, aged 59, was indicted for setting fire to some barns at Whittingstall, and a haystack at Harwood's Farm, in the parish of Watford, in this county, in May last. Mr. Petersdorff conducted the prosecution, Mr. Burney appeared for the prisoner.

The prisoner, it appeared, had been employed to catch rats on the premises in question, and had had some difference with the proprietor respecting the payment, and had declared his wish to see the place on fire. He was by his own admission in one of the barns when the fire broke out, having, as he said, lain down to sleep, but fled from the premises directly, being alarmed and unwell.

The Jury, after a short deliberation, found the prisoner Guilty.

His LORDSHIP passed sentence of death, which there is every probability will be carried into execution.

99. *An arson story – from The Times 14 July 1834. Baldwin was sentenced to death.*

98. *The Watford fire station in 1905. It stood in the High Street, where Gade House is now. Next door is the ivy-clad Upton House. The buildings were demolished in 1957.*

WATFORD'S CHARTER

Between 1850 and 1894 Watford was largely governed by a Board of Health, which was then replaced by an Urban District Council under the aegis of the Local Government Board. On 18 October 1922 Watford was granted Borough status. It was something for which Watford had long campaigned, certainly since the last decades of the 19th century, but the outbreak of the First World War had further delayed the arrival of Charter Day. Watford now had the right to build a Town Hall, make bye-laws and gain freedom from the Local Government Board. The first mayor was the Earl of Clarendon.

In the 1974 local government shake-up Watford become a district council within Hertfordshire, though continued as a borough, and the boundaries remained effectively the same.

LIBRARIES

The first public library was erected in Queen's Road. The money for the building was raised locally and it was opened by the Earl of Verulam in 1874. Needing extra space, a new library was built in 1928 with the help of the Carnegie Trust, at a cost of £20,000. This, the Watford Central Library, was further extended in 1961-3.

The North Watford branch library was built in 1937 on St Albans Road, and a mobile service was commenced in 1957.

THE TOWN HALL

Before Watford's incorporation as a borough, the council offices for many years had been at Upton House in the High Street. But after the 1922 Charter a town hall was built at the corner of Hempstead and Rickmansworth Roads. Designed by C. Cowles-Voysey, it was completed by 1939 at a cost of £186,000. Sir Thomas Beecham said of the main hall that it was one of the finest venues outside London for recording music.

100. Watford Central Library, built in 1928 with the help of the Carnegie Trust.

POOLS AND CENTRES

Watford has two swimming baths, one opposite the Town Hall – the Central Baths – and another in Leggatts Way. The Woodside Leisure Centre in Horseshoe Lane was opened by the Duke of Edinburgh on 4 November 1955. As well as there being an extensive community housing project, most of the estates have community centres operated by the council.

THE LOCAL PRESS

The first, and longest lasting, newspaper is the *Watford Observer*. Originally established in 1863 by Samuel Peacock, the paper has always prided itself on being a publication of local record. Originally situated on the corner of the High Street and Loates Lane, in 1961 the *Observer* moved to Rickmansworth Road, followed more recently to a new address in Watford Business Park.

Various Disorders

THE CHARTISTS IN WATFORD

Chartism was a working-class radical reform movement. Supporters were known as 'chartists' because twice they petitioned Parliament, once in 1839 and then again in 1842, for a Charter of Rights to reform and expand the franchise. Their aims were the enfranchisement of the male working class, the abolition of the property qualification for a seat in Parliament, equal representation, annual Parliaments, the payment of MPs, and voting by ballot.

On Monday 15 August 1842 approximately 2000 Chartists marched into Watford causing alarm amongst the inhabitants of this "quiet and retired town". *The Times* reported their arrival as shown in illustration 101.

A PRIZE FIGHT

We are told by the *Watford Observer* of 23 October 1863 of a disorderly occasion.

"On Wednesday last the peace of the neighbourhood was broken by a band of ruffians from London who came to participate in and witness a prize fight. We repeat – a prize fight – and a most disgusting sight it must have been if all is true we hear, not fit for publication. It appears the fight commenced at Tring and after the men had fought for an hour the police put a stop to it. They then took a train for Watford and on the train arriving they sprang from the carriages without showing their tickets and ran across the fields to Loates Lane, where in a meadow adjoining the lane a ring was formed and the fight renewed. The police made their appearance and did their best to stop the fight, but there only being two of them it was of no avail. Unfortunately our superintendent was out of town."

A public debate ensued as to the ability of the local police to handle such an occasion. The *Watford Observer* for 31 October 1863 commented that

"We are sorry to find that our police have got into trouble with regard to the prize fight that

CHARTIST CAMP MEETING AT WATFORD.—On Monday morning last the inhabitants of the quiet and retired town of Watford were thrown into considerable alarm by the appearance of a large body, about 2,000 in number, composed of both male and female Chartists, who entered the town through the railway arch, walking in procession, carrying flags and banners, and preceded by a band of music. They had arrived from London, whence they had been conveyed in about 80 vans, some drawn by two and others by four horses, in which they would have entered the town, had they not been stopped, about a mile off, by order of the magistrates, and told that the vans would not be allowed to go into Watford unless the banners were taken off. The whole in consequence descended, and determined to walk and carry the banners, &c., leaving the vans behind. The procession repaired to the Wheatsheaf, where they partook of some refreshment, and then dispersed in various groups to enjoy the neighbouring scenery ; they afterwards returned to dinner, which was laid out on the spacious bowling-green. At the conclusion of this repast, the whole body marched off to a field at the back of the town, whither they were followed by several agricultural and other labourers of the neighbourhood, and also by several farmers and others in gigs and on horseback. A hustings having been erected, Mr. Savage and several others addressed the meeting, urging the working men to join the Association in order to obtain the People's Charter as the only means by which they might expect to get a fair day's pay for a day's work. Three cheers were given for Feargus O'Connor and Mr. T. Duncombe, whose colours were carried at the head of the procession, and at the conclusion three cheers for the Charter. The present awfully distressed state of the country was much commented on, but scarcely any allusion made to the present disturbances. The party afterwards returned to the Wheatsheaf, where they were joined by several of the townspeople, and dancing commenced, which was kept up till long after the Chartists left to return to London, where they did not arrive till near midnight. Not the slightest disorder occurred. There were, however, 200 of the Hertford police stationed in the town in case of emergency, as the meeting was not wholly unlooked for from the circumstance of the Chartists having caused handbills to be posted and distributed through the town announcing their intention to make this rural excursion. The police, however, did not exhibit themselves. The procession was formed in Circus-street, New-road, London, and thence proceeded to their destination ; and to this circumstance may be attributed the absurd rumour which prevailed throughout the metropolis on Monday, that 2,000 Chartists had marched from London to Manchester and the disturbed districts.

101. From The Times *of 17 August, 1842, describing the Chartist gathering at Watford.*

took place on Wednesday week. In consequence of representations made to the Chief Constable, Captain Robertson, our superintendent, Mr. Hilsden, has been reduced to the rank of inspector with a consequent loss in salary amounting to £20 a year; Constable Coulter was ordered to be dismissed from the force and the wages of Constable Farr have been reduced to four shillings per week... Now we think it would be admitted that nothing but a gross dereliction of duty would warrant such a punishment as this. That such disgusting and brutalizing scenes as took place at Watford on Wednesday week should be put down by the arm of the law we must heartily affirm, and if the police have been guilty of negligence and cowardice it is right that such misconduct should not be passed over without reproof and punishment. Let us look, however, at the facts and see whether they deserve such severe measures being adopted towards one of the most efficient superintendents that we have ever had and towards two constables who have hitherto borne an excellent character in the police force... The two policemen Coulter and Farr, who were the only two members of the force available, endeavoured to stop the fight. The ruffians, using the most horrible oaths and imprecations, threatened their lives if they dared to interfere, and the policemen, seeing how great were the odds against them, gave up the attempt as hopeless. We cannot blame them for doing so; policemen are not expected to show superhuman courage in the discharge of their duties.'

A SCENE AT WATFORD.—There was a riot at Watford on Thursday night, and the shop of Mr. Bradley, a draper in the High-street, was wrecked by an excited mob. The excitement was occasioned by the suicide of Mr. Bradley's apprentice, a young woman about 17, named Newman, who left the shop on Monday evening, and was not seen until her body was found in the river Colne, at the back of Mr. Mead's flour-mill, on Wednesday morning. About half-past 7 on Thursday night, a mob assembled in front of Mr. Bradley's shop. Stones and other missiles were thrown at the windows of the shop and at the private house adjoining. At one time, later on in the evening, there must have been 2,000 persons present. After the shutters had been shattered, the plate-glass windows shared a similar fate, and in the end the fronts of the two houses were completely wrecked. None of the goods were stolen. The police were powerless. The Hon. Reginald Cappel, one of the local magistrates, made an unsuccessful attempt to read the Riot Act, and it was between 12 and 1 o'clock on Friday morning before the crowd dispersed. The work of destruction was confined entirely to Mr. Bradley's property. Yesterday afternoon a special meeting of the local magistrates was held, and several special constables sworn in. A number of police have arrived from the surrounding neighbourhood. The magistrates have cautioned the inhabitants against riotously assembling together. Though large numbers of persons assembled on Friday in front of Mr. Bradley's premises, no further damage was done, and none is apprehended now.

102. *The Watford riots of 1879. From* The Times *of 11 October.*

THE WATFORD RIOT 1902

In 1879, a Mr. Bradley, a draper with a shop in the High Street was suspected of having been involved in the death of his 17-year-old assistant, and was on the receiving end of a 2000-strong missile throwing crowd. Though the police were powerless the riot eventually fizzled out.

THE WATFORD RIOTS.
At the Watford Petty Sessions, yesterday, a full Bench of magistrates had before them 51 cases arising out of the riots on the previous Thursday. The chairman, before the cases were called on, said that they deplored the rioting which had taken place. The Bench wished to thank the special constables for the assistance they had rendered, and they could also commend Superintendent Wood, chief of the Watford police, for his conduct under very trying circumstances. Mr. J. H. Murphy appeared to prosecute for the Treasury, and, in his opening address, said that undoubtedly the riots were preconcerted, and did not arise in a haphazard manner. The prisoners were then tried in batches, the charges of larceny being taken first. Two women who were seen picking up and putting into a cloth boots which were being thrown out of one of the shops by the rioters were each sentenced to a month's hard labour. In the cases where goods were found when the police searched houses fines of £2 or 30s. were inflicted. The defence of this section of the prisoners was that they picked up the goods and intended to return them. The charges of malicious and wilful damage were taken next. A number of men of the labouring class received sentences ranging from two months' to one month's hard labour. When 31 cases had been dealt with, the Bench adjourned for the day. Among the cases which will be taken at the next sitting is one of arson, the prisoner being a youth named Clark, who is alleged to have fired the shop of Mr. Fisher.

103. *The Watford Riots of 1902, described in* The Times *of 2 July.*

Another riot occurred in 1902 because of what now seem to be remarkably trivial circumstances.

The people of Watford were looking forward to the celebrations associated with the coronation of King Edward VII, due to take place on 26 June. Watford had planned a number of events which were to include a large bonfire and teas for all the children of the town. Unfortunately for both King Edward and Watford, the King found himself fighting for his life with appendicitis. A number of public meetings took place to discuss the cancellation of the celebrations, at which the 'rougher element' proceeded to make their displeasure known. The 26th of June was a hot and sultry, with few reporting for work. As the day progressed the mood became increasingly ugly with demands for compensation for the lack of festivities. It was not long before the blame was being laid squarely on the shoulders of the chairman of the Council, Councillor Francis Fisher and that night a large crowd gathered in Watford and proceeded to break into and loot the shops of members of the coronation committee which included Mr Fisher, a local butcher. Four mounted policemen of the Hertfordshire Police were injured in the riot. In addition, thirty men from the Metropolitan Police were called in but arrived too late. It took 200 special constables, sworn in on the same evening, to put down the riot.[1] The *Watford Observer* had this to say:

Rioters bring shame to town

JUNE 28, 1902: Nothing so utterly disgraceful has occurred in Watford as the riot which took place on Thursday night and continued into the early hours of Friday morning.

During the day the Chairman of the Urban Council and other members of the Coronation Festivities Committee had been threatened by men because, forsooth, through the illness of our King, the bonfire was not to be lighted, and the giving of the dinner to the poor and the shilling which had been subscribed for by the promoters of the festivities for the children was to be postponed.

It is scarcely necessary to say that such men were eagerly joined by the sturdy young roughs of different parts of the town and with that kind of organisation which a mob employs, as the evening closed in, they assumed a threatening attitude in the Market-place. Soon after 9 o'clock they proceeded to the field where the bonfire was built. The fire was soon lighted, and then came the destruction of the fences and any property the mob could lay hands on.

With this they should have been content, but having, as it were, 'tasted blood', they made

their way to the Market-place and laid siege to the shop and premises of Mr. Fisher, the Chairman of the Urban District Council, who has endeavoured to do so much not only for the momentary celebration but for the permanent good of the town. Mr. Fisher defended his house in the best way he could.

The shop of Mr. Longley in the Market-place and that lower down the street next received attention and others near were, of course, damaged. The mob even proceeded so far as to set fire to Mr. Fisher's shop, a proceeding which shows the character of the leaders of the gang who started the mischief.

In the face of such a mob the police available were inadequate, and the affair went on until with the appearance of the firemen it became possible, by swearing in special constables, to get a sufficient body of peace-loving subjects to join hands and sweep the roughs from the streets.

This was ultimately accomplished, and a large number of arrests were made. Among those who were taken to the Police Station are a number who have suffered for their folly by bodily injury. Having brought it upon themselves they have little cause to complain.

Due precautions will be taken to prevent a recurrence of this foolish and disloyal conduct, which nine-tenths of the inhabitants regard with shame.

1   See Osborn, Neil, 'The Story of the Hertfordshire Police', *Hertfordshire Countryside*, 1969.

Drinking Places

PROSPEROUS BREWERS

An inhabitant of the nearby parish of Bushey commented at the end of the 19th century that

'....Our imports are large in quantity, but not numerous. We import in fact, but one article and that is beer. Our parish is rich in beer shops; I suppose we have one for every two families. The public houses and beer shops are an ornament to our parish.... Our beer is chiefly supplied from the neighbouring town of Watford, there are three or four brewers established there... The brewers all live in good style; they keep carriages and hunters, they fare sumptuously every day, and leave large fortunes to their children. Our parish are their principal customers. The publicans who drink the beer soon die, and wise people are supplied from London.'[1]

Watford was also renowned for the high ratio of pubs to population. A description of the town from the 1830s points out the "long straight street, the chief peculiarity of which was that about every third house seemed to bear the sign of a tavern, hotel, or ale-house." By the latter part of that century the High Street alone contained 42 drinking establishments and as late as the 1940s there were more than twenty pubs between Bushey Arches and the Market Place.[2]

Many of the old pub names and hotels were destroyed in the expansion in the 1970s of central Watford. However, some names are too important in the town's history to be ignored.

THE ROSE & CROWN

Henry Williams in the 1880s, lists five hotels in Watford. These were the Clarendon Hotel, the Essex Arms, the Rose & Crown, the Malden and the Verulam. Of these, the Rose & Crown and the Essex Arms, both situated in the High Street, were the focus of Watford life for centuries. The Rose & Crown originated in the 16th century and was primarily a coaching inn. Numerous reports in *The Times* from the late 18th century and through the course of the 19th century refer to it as being the host of criminals and disreputable types. It probably reached the peak of its notoriety when it became the hand-over point of a packaged corpse in a well-known body-snatching case in 1828 *(see p58).*

104. *Watford's 'notorious' Rose & Crown, before its demolition c.1954.*

The Rose & Crown was also known for the size of its landlord, a Mr James Rogers. We are told that

"a large business was done, many persons visiting the hotel for the purpose of seeing and conversing with its gigantic landlord. His exact weight does not appear to have been known, but some idea of his enormous size may be formed from the following particulars, which have been furnished by two or three old persons now residing at Watford who knew him well, one of them having been in his service as potboy. That he might take air, a chaise was built for him, very strong, with low wheels, and the bottom just off the ground, in which he was drawn about by a powerful pony, attracting at once the attention of persons in the street…His stomach was so large that, to enable him to take food at table with his family, a piece, half-circular in shape, was cut out of the table, and then by placing the dishes on either side of him he was enabled to take his food with tolerable comfort. He was a great eater, and when invited out to dine he would eat the greater part of a shoulder of mutton with a corresponding quantity of vegetables and bread before he left home, so that a moderate meal might suffice and prevent his host looking upon him as a gourmand… His size increased with his age, so that for a considerable time before his death on 10 June 1829, he was confined to a room on the ground floor, where he slept and took his food. In this room he died, and the undertaker had some difficulty in getting the coffin into the room, and when his body was put in it, greater difficulties presented themselves, for the weight was so

105. *The One Crown public house at 156 High Street, Watford's oldest pub, in 2005. It is Grade II listed.*

great that it required a larger number of men to carry the coffin than could get under it, and the doorway was so inconveniently situated that it could not be got out that way. After considerable deliberation the difficulty was overcome by taking out the window and frame and removing some of the brickwork, when several men using planks and levers got the coffin on to a low brewer's dray – lent for the occasion by Mr. Dyson, one of the brewers of the town – and it was drawn to the grave by the servants at the hotel.'[3]

Queen Victoria is credited with having changed the horses to her carriage here. By the latter part of the 19th century, under the proprietorship of John Read, the hotel had become the "rendezvous of noblemen, private gentlemen, commercial travellers, sportsmen, farmers and others from all parts of the country."

Livestock was sold weekly behind the Rose & Crown, but it was mostly known for being a staging point of the London stagecoach services.

THE ESSEX ARMS

The Essex Arms was a direct rival. Sited almost opposite in the High Street, its employees, as did those of the Rose & Crown, wore a distinguishing uniform. The Essex was also a staging inn through the centuries, as well as functioning as the local magistrates' court during the first half of the 19th century. It was at the Essex Arms that John Thurtell and his accomplice, Joseph Hunt were interrogated and detained after committing a murder in nearby Radlett *(see p.91)*. The balcony, which protruded from the first floor over the pavement, was a focal point for many centuries "for those wishing to make political speeches or address public meetings". It is said that W E Gladstone (four times British Prime Minister, last time 1894) made a speech from this vantage point while passing through the town. Perhaps the most notable event was the reading of the Riot Act in Watford from this balcony in 1902 *(see p. 101)*.[4]

The Essex Arms was demolished in the 1920s.

In 1756 the One Crown was kept by a Jeremiah Friend, and by 1844 it was owned by a Watford brewer, Edmund Fearnley Whittingstall. It is believed to be the oldest surviving public house in Watford.[5]

THE WHEATSHEAF

The Wheatsheaf was one of Watford's most famous public houses. The ancient pub sat at the lower end of the High Street near the tollgate that lay between Watford and Bushey. During the 18th and 19th centuries one of its barns was used as a theatre. It was knocked down and replaced with a pub of the same name in 1930. The new pub, at 312 High Street, sat further back from the road, but even this is now no more. Henry Williams describes the inn as it was in the 1830s.

"The Wheatsheaf Inn did a large trade about fifty years ago; indeed, it was looked upon as one of the principal inns of the town, and was the rendezvous of a number of the tradesmen, who frequently spent their evenings there. By the side of the house were pretty grounds, or what were then termed tea-gardens, where, under the shade of well-trained trees and filbert stems, seats and tables were fixed for the accommodation of young couples and other customers, who visited the place in large numbers on summer evenings, especially on Sunday evenings, and indeed on Sunday afternoons also, when hilarity, sometimes of a noisy nature, occasionally accompanied by the strains of a violin, was indulged in unrestrained, the law prohibiting such conduct on Sundays being at that time very unsatisfactory."

Parts of the Wheatsheaf's grounds were used for other purposes.

"There was a blacksmith's shop in the yard and stables. Later, in 1915 Richard Darlow had his wheelwright business on the site before taking over as landlord in 1923... In 1919 about three-quarters of the site was sold to Watford Engineering. The barn was gone but the stables remained. By 1928 the orchard and cottages associated with the Wheatsheaf had also gone and in 1930 and 1931 the rebuilding as a pub and the widening of the main road took place."

106. The George Inn Yard, now demolished, from a photograph of September 1894.

A MISERABLE WATFORD INN

Not everyone remembered their visit to Watford with fondness. Horace Walpole visited 'Cashiobury' and Moore-Park in July 1744 and observed, "dined miserably at a miserable inn at Watford and came home tired. I'll go no more of these journeys...'[6]

In the 1840s, a pub called The Fighting Cocks existed in Water Lane, where, indeed, cock fighting took place. The same pub also rented out rowing boats on the River Colne, regardless of how inebriated the customers were. A mid-nineteenth century report says that "the house and premises were generally crowded on Sunday afternoons and evenings, and not unfrequently a spill into the water occurred when the boat was occupied by youths who had indulged freely in drinking before they had started on their voyage up the Colne."

TEMPERANCE

The availability of cheap gin and beer in the 18th century led to a dramatic increase in the amount of drunkenness and its attendant social and health problems. Something had to be done. The Temperance movement was born in 1829 in Scotland and rapidly crossed the border. At the same time, 'Tee Total' societies arose promoting abstinence. The movement originally concentrated on the evils of gin before, around 1850, turning its attention to beer.

By the last quarter of the 19th century Watford boasted 5 breweries and 70 public houses – it was fertile ground for Temperance enthusiasts. Henry Kingham, a Baptist and dynamic force in the movement, created the Watford and Bushey Temperance Society, which was run in association with the Blue Ribbon Army. It managed to secure 8000 pledges – commitments to abstain from alcohol. In 1883 a nine-day Gospel Temperance Mission was held in Watford's Agricultural Hall that resulted sometimes in rowdy scenes:

"...there was much opposition to the temperance movement, and many persons, especially young men, attended the meetings for the purpose of making a disturbance, which they did by knocking the wooden walls with sticks or their fists, and stamping on the floor. Temperance work was very up-hill work then, and made but little progress, notwithstanding there were many earnest workers connected with that society."[7]

The Temperance movement faded after the First World War, though the problem of excessive drinking did not. In 1955 the British Temperance Society was formed in Watford at Stanborough Park, with the rather quaintly stated aim to urge people "by precept and example, by voice, by pen and by vote, to oppose the liquor traffic and discourage the use of intoxicants, tobacco and narcotics."

1   Groves, Tim *et al, From the Wheatsheaf to the Windmill: the story of Bushey and Oxhey pubs*, p10 (1984)

2   Watford WEA, *Aspects of Nineteenth Century Watford* p5 (1987)

3   Williams, p157 (1884)

4   Gloag, Mr J, 'Reminiscences of Watford'

5   Castle, Stephen, *Timber-Framed Buildings in Watford* p14 (1977)

6   Toynbee, Paget Jackson and Toynbee, Helen, *The Letters of Horace Walpole, Fourth Earl of Orford* (1903)

7   Williams p169

Industrial Watford

THE SILK INDUSTRY

Silk spinning originated in Watford in the 18th century and is listed in 1792 as the principal industry of the town.

Defoe in his *A Tour Through the Whole Island of Great Britain*, published in 1778 wrote,

"Upon the river is a large silk manufactory, which is three stories high, and has thirty-three sash windows on each side; it employs an hundred persons, and belongs to *Thomas Deacon, Esq*; who lives in the town."

He would be one of the numerous Thomas Deacons (all first sons were called Thomas) who lived at Wiggen Hall. *The Universal British Directory* of 1792, describes Watford's industry as follows:

"The principal manufactory of this town is throwing of silk, and for which there are three different buildings, two worked by horses and one by water. That which is worked by water is by far the largest. The river Colne runs at the back of Watford town, and through the bottom thereof; and, turning a little may be seen from the houses on the other side of the town, and may be said in part to surround the town, in the vicinity of which it turns four mills, viz, a paper-mill belonging to Mr. Lewin, called Bushey-mill; a flour-mill in the town of Watford, occupied by Mr. Henry Field; the silk-mill, occupied by Mr. Paumier; and a paper mill, occupied by Mr. Lepard, which is called Hamper-Mill."

It would be interesting to know if Mr Lepard was involved in the founding of the 18th-century firm of London paper merchants, Lepard & Smith, which still survived in the 1970s.

The Rookery Mill at the lower end of the town was the largest silk factory employing 500 persons in the 1790s. The mill ceased in 1881.

In the early 1800s one silk mill is listed as being at the top end of Red Lion Yard off the High Street, and owned by a Mr Toppin. Another in the 18th century was opposite the pond. Another, described as an old wooden

A fire lately broke out about five in the morning in the flour mill at Watford, about three miles on the other side Hertford; which in little more than two hours entirely confumed the mill, ftables, warehoufes, &c. together with grain, meal, and other property to a large amount.— Mr. Geare, foreman of the mill, and mafter of a public-houfe nearly adjoining, the only dwelling within a mile of the fpot where the accident happened, had nearly loft his life in an ineffectual attempt to fave his employer's books ; for he was fo near being fuffocated, that he was dragged out by his own fon not fo much as a minute before the whole roof fell in, being in a ftate of total infenfibility. However, in a fhort time after being in the air, Mr. Geare recovered.

107. *From* The Times *6 April, 1790*

mill worked by a water-wheel, stood at the bottom of the High Street.

Despite all the evidence of industrial activity, Josiah Conder, resident in the 1830s, seems not to be aware of it, for in his memoirs written at exactly the same time as the arrival of the railway, to him Watford is still a sleepy country town. It possessed, he says:

"the usual features and social elements of a small market-town in an agricultural district, with no staple trade or manufacture... there was the dissenting minister who preached at the quaint little old Baptist chapel... there were two or three rival lawyers, and two or three rival doctors, and two rival principal inns, one with a gentlemanly landlord, the other with an unparalleled waiter. There was the retired great book-seller, and the great brewer preparing to retire, and the great nobody, at the great white house, and the great man, who drove about in a little chaise, because he was too bulky to walk, never went to church because he could not get into his pew, and was credibly reported always to eat a leg of mutton as a precaution before he went out to dine. There were rich millers and farmers, and well-to-do shopkeepers, and hard-working cottagers, too many publicans, and a full average of beggars and scamps."

Williams tells us that, "In 1831 straw plait was manufactured here in large quantities, and there were three silk-throwsting mills, eight malt kilns, and two extensive breweries." By the time Samuel Lewis published his *Topographical Dictionary of England* in that year we can see a subtle shift in the emphasis of industry. The Grand Union Canal (then the Grand Junction) which passed through both Cassiobury Park and The Grove was fully functional allowing the transportation of goods from the Thames right through to Birmingham. The industrial revolution was underway and the breweries were now becoming increasingly prominent. Lewis speaks of:

"The manufacture of straw-plat, and three silk-throwsting mills, employ a considerable number of persons; there are likewise eight malt-kilns, and two extensive breweries."

An 'Old Inhabitant' writing at the end of the 1870s mentions that

"A large Silk Mill and two Paper Mills give employment to several hundreds of the population; there are also two Breweries, and several Malt Kilns."[1]

The decription in John Bartholomew's 1887 *Gazetteer of the British Isles* is business like:

"**Watford**.— market town and par., Herts, in SW. of co., on river Colne, 9 miles SW. of St Albans and 18 miles NW. of London by rail – par., 10,780 ac., pop. 15,507; town (comprising parts of Bushey and Watford pars.), 530 ac., pop. 10,073; P.O., T.O., 2 banks, 2 newspapers. Market-day, Tuesday. Watford has an ancient parish church, free library, and school of science and art. In the town and neighbourhood are a silk factory, straw-plait factory, wood-turning works, breweries, papermills, and some other industrial establishments. The London Orphan Asylum is situated at Watford."

By the end of the 19th century, Watford was becoming much more varied in the make-up of its industry. The silk mills and straw-plaiting were a nostalgic memory and modern industry was making its mark. There were breweries, a steam laundry, a cold storage company and large works for colour printing and engraving. "On the east side of the railway, along the line

On Friday night or early on Saturday morning the paper-mill belonging to Mr. LEPARD, near Watford, Herts, was entirely consumed by fire. The dwelling-house and premises for the workmen being separate are no ways damaged; happily no lives are lost.

108. From The Times 7 January 1793.

of the road to St Albans, the district of Callowland is extending in a similar manner, the factories there include large cocoa works and several printing and colour process works..."

PRINTING

Apart from its breweries, the major industry in Watford was printing. John Peacock opened a printing works in 1823, in Lower High Street, and Watford Museum contains a Columbian printing press which was made in 1820 and arrived in Watford around 1823 for his use. It printed the first copy of the *Watford Observer* on 24 January 1863, by which time it was owned by Samuel Peacock who had his office in what is now Queens Road.

The 20th century saw printing overtake brewing as the predominant industry. By the 1960s thousands were employed in the many firms in Watford, but the two key companies were Odhams and the Sun Engraving Company. The fraudulent activities of Robert Maxwell, their owner, had a disastrous effect on these businesses, causing many thousands of Watford residents to lose their pensions.

Odhams had begun in a modest way in Covent Garden in 1894, founded by the Odhams brothers. At a low ebb in this small business they took on, as office boy, Julius Salter Elias, who, within a year, was made manager. He was an obsessive and meticulous worker and, realising that the only way to make the business pay was to have regular contract work, he set out with much success to attract magazine printing. Publications such as *Racing Pigeon* and *Vanity Fair* were printed in Floral Street and the firm expanded nearby. The turning point in the firm's history was the contract to print the controversial *John Bull*, owned by the maverick MP Horatio Bottomley. Eventually Odhams

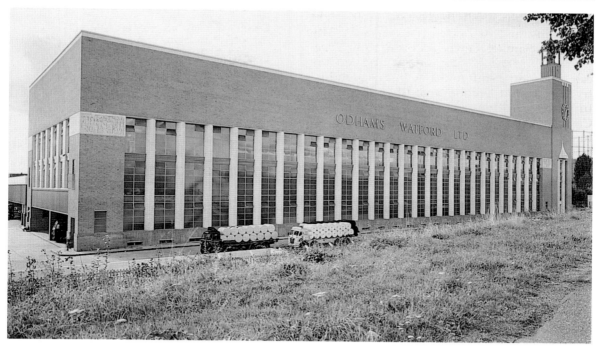

109. *The Odhams building at Watford, designed by Sir Owen Williams in 1937. It closed in 1983.*

110. *Linotypes in operation at Odhams.*

111. *Benskin's Brewery.*

bought that magazine and invented its own – such as *Ideal Home, Picturegoer* and many others, especially for the growing women's readership. All this could not be contained in Covent Garden, and the firm opened what was then the biggest printing works in England in Watford, pioneering the use of photogravure printing.

WATFORD'S BREWERIES

Brewing developed in Watford and surrounding villages from a cottage industry to something quite integral to Watford by the mid 19th century. In the 17th century hops were grown in nearby Rickmansworth, and that century also saw the growth of what is termed 'the common brewer' or brewer who supplied several inns, as opposed to the innkeepers who brewed their own beer. At this time common brewers realised that by owning the inns, they could guarantee their sales, and by the end of the 19th century breweries owned the majority of the local inns and beer houses.

As concern increased about the quality of water used in London breweries, the firms looked for alternative sources. Watford was one of the Hertfordshire towns which fitted the bill.

John Day is the first brewer we know of in Watford, in 1619. In 1635 there is a mention of the sale of a brew-house, malt-house, mansion and inn and in 1636 a Nicholas Colborne, a Watford brewer is noted.[2]

In 1750 the Cannon Brewery in Watford High Street was under the ownership of John Dyson who farmed and grew his own barley. A later John Dyson and his brother Ralph, having successfully developed the business, sold it to Joseph Benskin in 1867. Benskin rebuilt the brewery and by 1872 was producing 9000 gallons of ale a week. After Benskin's death in 1877 his widow, son, and son-in-law took over eight rival local breweries increasing production over the course of the next 20 years to 45,000 gallons a week. "A full train was loaded every working day. The Grand Union canal was also used, with shipments from Cassio Wharf to London Docks and thence to the Continent especially during the Great War." [3]

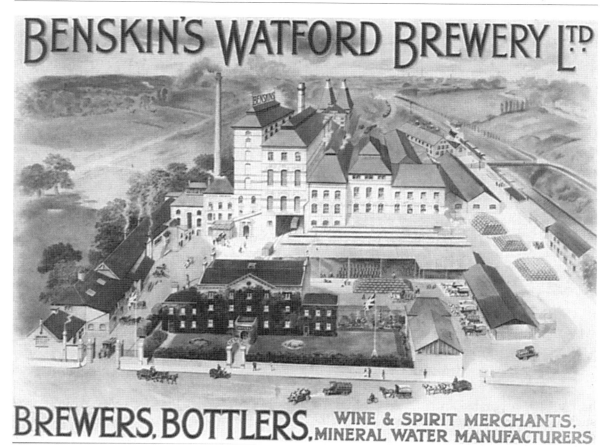

BENSKIN'S WATFORD BREWERY L^{TD.}

BREWERS, BOTTLERS, WINE & SPIRIT MERCHANTS, MINERAL WATER MANUFACTURERS

112. A poster advertising Benskin's c.1920.

Concern over the number of brewery-control-led public houses is apparent from a House of Commons report as early as 25 May 1822. A Mr H Bennet had presented a petition from "a large and respectable body of licensed victual-lers" complaining of the methods used in al-lowing the licensing of public houses. The pro-ceedings, printed in *The Times,* assert that in Watford all public houses were controlled either by magistrates or brewers.

Healey's Brewery of Watford founded *c.* 1820 by George Healey stood in King Street, with an entrance in George Street. Benskin's bought the brewery in 1898. Sedgwick's brewery was ac-quired by John Fellowes Sedgwick in 1862 and,

113. The Cannon Brewery.

114. Staff at Benskin's Brewery c. 1900.

perhaps inevitably, succumbed to Benskin's in 1923. Sedgwick's, under Frederick Sedgwick, introduced the first steam operated fire engine to Watford in 1876. Frederick seems to have been an interesting character, as his "energy and flamboyance also found an outlet in 1873 when he took a leading part in the nostalgic revival of the stage-coach."[4]

1   'Old Inhabitant' *A Guide to Hertfordshire, with a History and Description of the Various Towns and Villages,* p361 (1880)

2   Saunders p29

3   Groves, Tim, *et al, From the Wheatsheaf to the Windmill: The Story of Bushey and Oxhey Pubs,* p17 (1984)

4   *Ibid,* p25

The High Street

For much of Watford's recorded history the High Street *was* Watford. Today the street is a busy and modern place, dominated by the Harlequin shopping centre, but unfortunately the wholesale destruction which took place in the 1970s to allow its construction almost totally obliterated any relationship of the present with the past. However, some buildings dating back to the 16th century survive.

Daniel Defoe in the 1778 edition of *A Tour through the Island of Great Britain* described Watford as a "genteel markate town... very long, having but one street", and this description pertained until after the arrival in 1838 of the London & North Western Railway.

In the 1830s the vistas are described as charming, "embracing the High Street, Church, Watford Place, Cannon Brewery, and surrounding houses, with several green pastures, clumps of trees, and other vegetation. On these natural seats fishermen patiently sat for hours, enjoying not only the sport to be obtained there but the exhilarating air and fine prospect around."[1] And, as we have seen,[2] the 1849 Report of the General Board of Health, described Watford as "composed of a principal street, about one and a half miles long."

It was a very quiet town. A resident's memoir of 1902 noted that "In my young days you could have fired a cannon ball down the High Street and have hit no one – everybody was in doors after dark and the shutters up."[3]

A description of 1880 noted that "At the bottom, near the railway bridge, stood the toll-house, a square building of two floors, hanging from the front of which was a lantern that, before the introduction of gas, contained a small oil lamp..."

Greater development of the High Street came in the 1850s when Queens Road was developed on the east side to lead down to the station. At the same time King Street was developed on the west side. King Street also marked

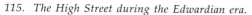

115. The High Street during the Edwardian era.

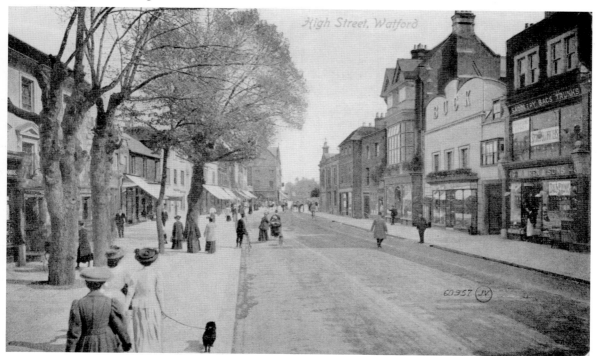

116.   *The High Street c. 1840. The Essex Arms is on the left, the Rose & Crown on the right, and in the distance in front of the church tower is the old Market Hall, which was destroyed by a fire in 1853.*

the original carriage driveway for Watford
Place. In 1855 the Corn Exchange was built in
the High Street, replacing the market house
destroyed by fire in 1853.

At the turn of the twentieth century it was
still possible to describe the High Street as
retaining modernity and charm. Cassio hamlet
lay at the north end where the library stands
today. The Cassiobury Dower House, an 18th-
century dwelling built by a former Earl of Essex,
is there.

The *Victoria County History* volume of 1902
that deals with Watford, describes the High
Street:

"...Proceeding south, at the junction of St
Albans Road with High Street is the Elms so-
called from the fine old trees in front. It was
formerly known as Townend House, and has
been rebuilt within recent years. A little beyond
are two houses known as Monmouth House

117. *Ballard's Buildings, off the High Street, some of
Watford's worst slums, shown here in 1898.*

118. The High Street, a photograph taken 8 September 1903, looking towards the north, at around no. 186.

119. The High Street in the 1930s.

120. The High Street c. 1920 with the draper's, Cawdell & Co. and the Essex Arms Hotel in view. Neither has survived. The Essex Arms was in fact demolished to make way for an extension of the Cawdell building.

and The Platts. They originally formed one house which was built by Robert Carey, Earl of Monmouth (then residing at Moor Park, Rickmansworth), early in the seventeenth century, as a dower house. After his death in 1639 his widow lived here until her own death three years later, when the property was sold. Soon after 1771 the house was divided into two, and about the year 1816 the then owner altered the portion now known as Monmouth House, cementing the front, and entirely altering its appearance. The other part, The Platts, is however, in pretty much its original condition. It is a brick building with two steep gables to the street, and has massive projecting chimneys at the end. Though very simple and quite devoid of ornament it is a very pleasing and well-proportioned building of the period. The interior has been a good deal altered, but in the

dining room the walls have wooden panelling, and there is a good oak moulded chimney-piece reaching up to the ceiling. The old stair is of oak, and is of small dimensions, with massive moulded newels, but, like the other woodwork in the house, unrelieved by carving. Between Monmouth House and the south end of the market place there is very little old work of interest, with the exception of a small oak traceried window of fifteenth-century work, which was discovered during alterations, and refixed in the outer wall of the 'Compasses' public house at the corner of Market Street.

At the south end of the market place are two small houses, at the back of which, in Church Street, is a well-carved oak barge-board, pierced and foliated, probably of sixteenth-century work. In an alley off Church Street is a block of houses known as Ballard's Buildings, now

The Pond, Watford

121. The pond c. 1905.

inhabited by very poor families, which has an early eighteenth-century brick front with some good moulded brickwork, and a wooded hood with carved brackets over the entrance.

On the south side of the churchyard is the Free School, an interesting brick building with stone quoins, which has a good open bell-turret of wood on the roof. The school was built in 1704 and endowed in 1708... In one of the class rooms is a fine oak chimney piece, which appears to belong to the late Elizabethan period, and which must have been brought from elsewhere. Adjoining the Free School is the present vicarage with a central block and east and west wings, partly of timber construction. In the west wing is some good early seventeenth-century woodwork, and parts of the house may well be of yet older date. Behind is a pretty old-fashioned garden. At the back of this is the old vicarage, one of the most interesting old buildings left in Watford. It is situated in Fenn's Yard, off High Street. It is a two-storied building of timber plastered on the

outside, and has a plain brick chimney and a tiled roof... There are still a number of interesting eighteenth-century brick fronts in High Street, in many cases having wood and plaster buildings of picturesque appearance behind them. No. 97, High Street has good brick pilasters with Ionic capitals, and until recently it possessed a fine moulded brick cornice. A little way down Water Lane, on the east side of High Street, is an old cottage, with the upper part of the front weather-boarded, which has a brick chimney with moulded string. At the foot of High Street, on the west side, is Farthing Lane, which contains some picturesque old lath-and-plaster cottages with gables, and a little farther down High Street, on the same side, is a house now divided into shops and dwelling houses, which has a good seventeenth-century chimney-stack, and an old wooden mantelpiece and some panelling inside. Opposite this, the old 'Angel' projects its timbered upper story over the pavement, while just beyond is some good eighteenth-century in Grove Place."[4]

122. A hundred years later – Watford Pond at the northern end of the High Street. Photo 2005.

Ballard's Buildings had been used in the 1830s to house railway workers. These were demolished in 1926 under a slum clearance order.

Stephen Castle states in his foreword to *Timber-Framed Buildings in Watford* (1977) that in 1950 the town centre could boast 121 historic buildings.

THE HIGH STREET TODAY

At first glance the High Street appears to be almost devoid of Watford's past. This is anything but the case. Watford Museum offers weekly guided tours of the High Street, which have proved increasingly popular. The street still retains a large number of historic Grade II listed buildings dating back to the 16th-century as well as a number of curiosities.

Proceeding north along the High Street, Moss's sits on the corner with Market Street. Embedded in the side wall in Market Street is a 15th-century window removed from the Old Compasses inn, itself demolished in 1928. The window is believed to have belonged originally to a rest house that stood on the site for the benefit of visitors to Watford Market.

On the corner of the High Street and New Street is a 19th-century Coal Duty boundary marker. This is a good example of historic recycling as the marker was originally located by the canal at the railway arch over the River Colne. After the Great Fire of London an Act was passed enabling the City of London Corporation to levy duty on coal and wine to help rebuild the City, but the boundary marker pictured in illustration 126 would have been placed in 1851 after a further Act was passed. The duty was abolished in 1889.

137 High Street is a Grade II early 18th-century building. Nos. 137-139 on the corner of Carey Place were originally one building L-shaped in plan. Three bays of the front were rebuilt in red brick in *c.*1700. The ground floor has been completely gutted by the insertion of a modern shop and staircase. The first floor comprises three rooms, two of which are original, while the third and largest occupies that part of the structure rebuilt in *c.*1700.

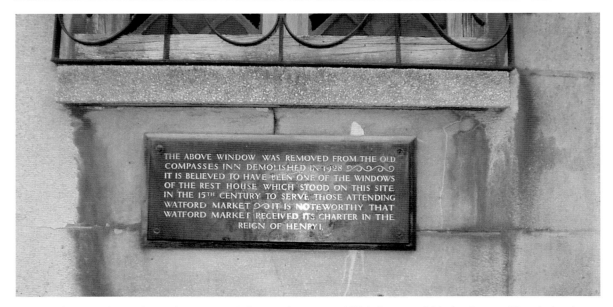

123. *A plaque underneath a 15th-century window on the corner of High Street and Market Street. The window is thought to have been part of a 'rest house' for those attending the market.*

124. *No. 139 High Street – the Tudor-framed building in the centre. Photo 2005.*

125. (Above) Monmouth House in 2005.

126. (Below) Coal Duty marker on the corner of New Street and High Street.

MONMOUTH HOUSE

Monmouth House, sits at the northern end of the High Street just to the south of the pond. When built, it stood in grounds which extended beyond the current railway line. It is a substantially early- to mid- 17th century red brick house built for Robert Carey, Earl of Monmouth who died in 1639. It was sold in 1771 and split into two. Further alterations took place in about 1816 when the northern end was refaced. The northern half was entirely rebuilt in 1927 to match the heavily restored southern half. The rebuilt parts are believed to include materials from Cassiobury House. This is highly possible as the demolished structure of Cassiobury House was sold for building purposes in that year.

1   Williams p73
2   Report to the General Board of Health, 1849, p4
3   H West, quoted by Saunders
4   *Victoria County History*, Hertfordshire, Vol. 2, pp 447, 448, 449

Ghostly Watford

JOCKEY FENSON

Henry Williams, in the late early 1880s, relates a story of Jockey Fenson, an inmate of the Pest House at around the end of the 18th century. Fenson committed suicide, and thus was barred from a Christian burial. He was instead buried in a dell in Hagden Lane, just before the turning for Tolpits. "Soon a rumour spread that a spectre clad in white walked the lane nightly, and might sometimes be seen sitting on the gates or gliding noiselessly over the adjoining fields, and a great fear seized the children of the town and neighbourhood; indeed, many adults refused to pass the dell or go anywhere near it. The perturbation of the people became so great that the parochial authorities had the body removed… it was re-buried at night in one corner of the old churchyard." Presumably the hauntings ceased.

TROUBLED SPIRITS

Williams tells us too of a number of unsettling incidents in the area of Feather Bed Lane, which has since been renamed Shady Lane. It was then a bridleway which ran from a point near the junction of Clarendon Road and the High Street to the bridge over the railway on the St Albans Road. The area has since been developed for housing.

Williams, though expressing a number of disclaimers, eagerly informs us that

"this lane was notorious, as it was said to be the rendezvous of the troubled spirits of departed persons, and many tales were told of strange sights that have been seen there, and occurrences that had taken place in its depths during the dark and silent hours of night. I remember, when a boy, [*c.* 1830s] a tale was current that a young man, not being satisfied with the conduct of his lover, obtained her promise to meet him in Feather Bed Lane one night at the hour of eleven, telling her he had something of very great importance to communicate to her, which was for her ears only. Unsuspecting, she went there at the appointed hour, but her lover had been detained, and, he not being there, she walked about, and presently saw by the light of the moon an open grave, recently dug under some overhanging bushes. The truth flashed upon her mind – he was going to murder her! She hastened from the lane, and thus her life was saved. Subsequently a person hung himself in this lane, and that stamped its character as a place where all kinds of unearthly sights might be seen and noises heard after the dread hour of twelve at night."

Williams then gives us a list of further sites which, it was believed, were 'troubled' such as a dell near the railway bridge, the railway tunnel, Hagden Lane and the churchyard. Several houses were also affected.

"The one now occupied by Mr. Downer, stationer, was untenanted for a very long time before he took it: the cause was said to be that it was haunted by the spirit of a lady who had previously resided there. More bold than some persons of that day, he took the house, and has enjoyed a residence there for many years, undisturbed by those unearthly visitations accredited to it."

Alan Ball in his *Street and Place Names in Watford* says that the area of Feather Bed Lane was sunk below the surrounding fields, and well endowed with foliage. He believes that

"the character of the bridleway made it natural that people should think of it at night as being the haunt of ghosts and evil spirits, and when the whole area was developed for housing, the short road between Clarendon and Westland Roads was called Shady Lane, probably as a reminder of its past. It is interesting to note in this connection, that to local people, the word 'shady' would have the double connotation of a place in shadow that by inference was the haunt of underhand or unpleasant happenings."

THE GHOST OF THE PALACE THEATRE

The Palace Theatre opened in 1908 as a music hall called the Watford Palace of Varieties. Although no actual figures have been witnessed here, the 'presence' of 'something unseen' has often been claimed and certainly experienced.

127. Watford Palace theatre – haunted by a 'presence' and 'something unseen'.

Mysterious footsteps have been heard occasionally crossing the stage, but phenomena seem to be located particularly in one dressing-room. Here the 'feeling' of someone is frequently felt and often accompanied by a drop in temperature, followed by a series of footsteps which stop at the door. Maintenance staff and two of the executives have admitted to hearing the sounds, created, they believe, by the ghost of a former stage-hand.[1]

HIGH STREET GHOSTS

Number 97 was reputedly haunted by an old lady resident and for many years after she died the building remained empty. Another High Street haunting is reputed to take place at 26a above Jackson's the jewellers. The building dates from the 15th century and there have

been a number of claims to have seen the apparition of an Elizabethan gentleman. He has been described as "an old man just over 5ft tall and wearing stockings, doublet and puffy short trousers and appears in a grey colourless mist-like form."[2]

Ruth Stratton and Nicholas Connell in their recent book, *Haunted Hertfordshire,* list a number of reputed ghostly activities, including objects being thrown at the window of the *Watford Observer* building, and the petrifying figure of a hooded monk making a strangling gesture to an unfortunate woman in Tudor Avenue. During the building of the railway tunnel

"through part of a churchyard near Watford...coffins fell open and human remains tumbled out onto the rail workers below. Once

128. *Jackson's the jewellers in the High Street, in one of the oldest buildings in Watford, 'haunted by an Elizabethan gentleman'.*

the line was finished, the steam engine drivers seemed to experience problems passing one particular point in the tunnel where a sudden, vicious blow-back caused several drivers severe burns. The point was traced as being where the line had cut into the churchyard."

AN APPROPRIATE SPIRIT – A CASSIOBURY PHANTOM

Of all the Watford apparitions listed by Ruth Stratton and Nicholas Connell, the most famous is that of Arthur, Lord Capel executed by Cromwell in 1649. Although he spent most of his earthly time at Hadham Hall, he has seen fit to return to Cassiobury where on moonlit nights, around 9 March, he may be seen roaming the pathways of Cassiobury Park. He has been variously described as having long hair and a full moustache, and sometimes as 'headless'.

THE PHANTOM OF THE GROVE

Unlike the long deceased Cassiobury, The Grove, the former home of the earls of Clarendon, is still very much present and boasts the re-enactment of a ghostly fox hunt. The phantom is that of Lord Doneraile, who it is said was condemned to "ride forever with hell hounds in pursuit of an equally phantom fox…" This bizarre re-enactment is Lord Doneraile's eternal punishment for converting an ancient chapel in the basement of the mansion into a kitchen when he built the Grove in the 18th century. A former warden claimed he saw the ghost on many occasions. He told the *Watford Observer* in 1974, "When we came here in 1957 they decided to do some alterations and when they took down some plaster in the present entrance lounge they discovered a font in the wall. It was pale blue and built into a wall 3ft thick.'[3]

1   Courtesy Andrew Green www.mystical-www.co.uk/ghost/zsee.htm

2   Stratton, Ruth and Connell, Nicholas, *Haunted Hertfordshire: A Ghostly Gazetteer* (2003) p226

3   *Ibid* p233

Leisure Times

HUNTING

With the presence of two very large landed estates, it was almost inevitable that Watford became involved in fox hunting. The two most prominent hunts to ride over the Cassiobury estate were the Salisbury and Berkeley Hunts. It is an indication of how rural Watford and its environs were in the first part of the 19th century that a Royal Deer Hunt was able to ride for three hours from Farnham, cross the Uxbridge Road, past Denham and end in Watford after 20 miles, with little difficulty (*see ill. 129*).

MAY DAY

Cussans writing in the 1870s[1] comments that the

> "custom of observing May Day still survives in Watford and its neighbourhood. Parties of children, fantastically dressed, parade the streets. In front are two children holding a stick between them, from which depends a garland of wild flowers, tied round with bits of gaudy ribbon. Of the song they sing, the following verses will give an idea:

Here begins the merry month of May,
The bright time of the year;
When Christ our Saviour died for us,
He loved us so dear.

We have been walking all the night,
And the best part of this day;
And now returning back again,
We bring you a branch of May.

A branch of May we have brought you,
And at your door it stands;
It is but a sprout, but its well budded out,
In the shape of our Lord's hands.

My song is done, and I must be gone,
No longer can I stay;
God bless you all, both great and small,
And send you a joyful May!

> ROYAL HUNT.—On Monday morning, soon after ten o'clock, a fine deer was turned out of the cart for the day's diversion at Salt-hill. The hunt was well attended by sportsmen of all ranks. The deer took at first across the fields by Farnham church, through Stoke-common and the woods and enclosures to the right of Bulstrode-park, crossed the Uxbridge-road, taking to the right by Denham. from thence he crossed the country towards Watford, and was at last taken near Lord Essex's park, after a hard run of upwards of three hours: very few sportsmen were in when taken. This is the course of country this deer always takes when turned out. It is about 20 miles from Salt-hill.

129. *From* The Times *8 November 1822.*

FOOTBALL

The first mention of football being played in Watford comes from an 1870 *Watford Observer* at a time when it was considered to be a nasty and brutish pastime. The *Observer* refers to 'Hertfordshire Rangers' who played in a meadow in Langley Road. This club, which received FA recognition in 1866, comprised mainly Aldenham, Elstree and Cambridge University players. Its captain, the son of the vicar of Rickmansworth, was selected for England. In 1875, Rangers became the first local side to compete in the Football Association Cup. The club disbanded in 1882.

Watford Rovers was formed in 1881 "by a group of young lads who had been given permission to kick a football about in Cassiobury Park..."[2] Henry Grover, a member of a prosperous local family was the founder of the club. He lived in Cassio Road and then Upton Road between 1906 and his death in 1949 and is buried almost opposite the Watford ground in Vicarage Road cemetery. Unlike the private jets and luxury transport of today's football clubs, transport in those early days to some of the more local away games was often undertaken by horse and cart by these middle class sons of Watford, and there are anecdotes about the players engaging in cherry-picking and a hostelry-crawl on the return journey. It was essentially a team comprising players from families who had made their mark financially in the area and were regarded as well-to-do. The Rovers became part of the West Herts Club at Cassio Road in 1890 and as West Herts joined the Southern League in 1896; they became professional the following year. In 1898

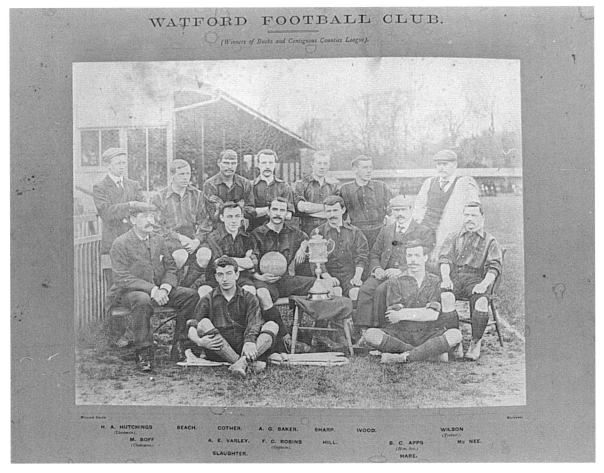

WATFORD FOOTBALL CLUB.

(Winners of Bucks and Contiguous Counties League).

H. A. HUTCHINGS	BEACH.	COTHER.	A. G. BAKER.	SHARP.	WOOD.	WILSON
(Linesman).						*(Trainer).*
M. BOFF		A. E. VARLEY.	F. C. ROBINS	HILL.		Mc NEE.
(Chairman).			*(Captain).*		B. C. APPS	
		SLAUGHTER.			*(Hon. Sec.)*	
					HARE.	

130. *Watford Football Club c. 1890.*

the name Watford Football Club was adopted and in 1900 it won the Division Two championship of the Southern League. In 1915 the club won that League's championship and five years later joined the Football League.

Watford had a number of ground changes over the years. These included the Rose and Crown Meadow, Colney Butts Meadow near the Watford Girls' Grammar School, then Cassio Road opposite where the Cassiobury Park Gates stood.

The Vicarage Road site, their present ground since 1922, was bought by the Benskin's brewing firm in 1921. The *Watford Observer* of August 1922 described the new ground as covering "6½ acres, and the total estimated accommoda-

tion is 33,000, for 5,000 of whom cover is provided. The grandstand will hold about 1,400, and there are two other stands. Commodious dressing-rooms are provided, together with bath-houses (including, shower baths); there are also a directors' room, cashier's room, referee's room and bath, a bar, and store rooms, and – as auctioneers say – the usual offices." The ground was opened on 30 August 1922 for a match (a goalless draw) with Millwall Athletic. Over 8,000 were present.

Throughout the 1930s Watford remained near the top of Division Three South, though it did reach the sixth round of the FA Cup in 1932. During the Second World War competitive football was suspended, resuming in 1946. In

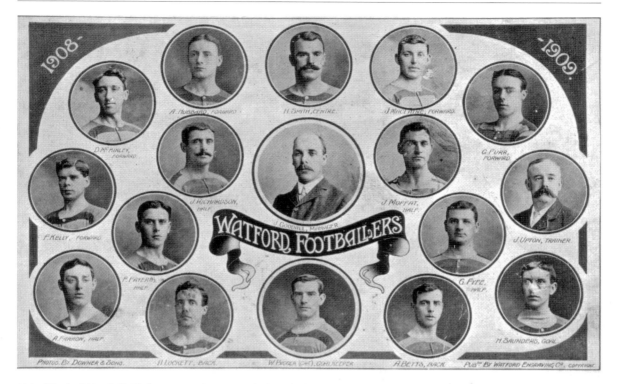

131. *Watford Football Club on an early postcard, during the 1908-09 season.*

132. *Football crowd at the Vicarage Road ground in the 1920s.*

133. Destiny nightclub now occupies the site of Hertfordshire's largest cinema, the Plaza, which became the Odeon.

1958 after 38 years in Division Three South, Watford became founder members of Division Four and in 1960 were promoted to Division Three. 1969 was a notable year when the 'Hornets' met Manchester United in the FA Cup, holding them to a draw in front of a crowd of 34,000, and gaining promotion to Division Two. The next year they reached the semi-final of the FA Cup, only to be defeated by Chelsea. Then came a low point in the Club's fortunes, and by 1975 it had been relegated down to Division Four again. But then, under the management of Graham Taylor and the chairmanship and largesse of pop-star Elton John, they stormed back up the League all the way to Division One in 1982. In 1984 the Club got to the FA Cup final, but lost to Everton.

Graham Taylor returned as manager in 1997-8 and in 1999 the club was in the Premiership for the first time.

The club is well known for having adopted a community approach to football and for promoting football for the 'family'. It was the first club to have a family enclosure.[3]

WATFORD'S CINEMAS

Moving pictures first came to Watford on 8 March 1897 at the Clarendon Hall. William F Jury's Imperial Bioscope Company paid its annual visit from 1905 to 1909. On 2 October 1909 the first permanent cinema opened at the Corn Exchange in Market Place (no longer there). Initially it was very successful, and having changed to the Electric Picture Palace in January 1914 it disappeared. Other early cinemas were films shown in the Palace Theatre in Clarendon Road from 1910. In 1911 the Cinema Palace at 134 High Street opened, failing by 1915. It stood near the corner of King Street. In 1912 the variously named Electric

Coliseum, Coliseum, and Plaza opened at 149 St Albans Road, on the corner of Bedford Street. This lasted intermittently until July 1954 when it closed, followed by demolition in 1957. In 1913 the Empire, and subsequently the ABC, Cannon, and again ABC, opened in Merton Road. It met the same fate as Watford's other cinemas, but having survived until 1996 it set the record as Hertfordshire's longest running cinema. 1913 also saw the opening of the Central Hall cinema at 19-21 King Street on the corner of Granville Road. This cinema was graced on its opening night with the presence of the Earl of Clarendon. It subsequently became the Regal, and finally the Essoldo, becoming an unusual cinema for Watford – a survivor. In 1921 at 44 High Street came the Bohemian. This lasted only four weeks and the site is now occupied by The Moon Under Water public house. 1921 also saw the arrival of the Super, later the Carlton at 24 Clarendon Road, adjoining the Palace Theatre. It was the first cinema in Watford, from December 1928, to show talking pictures. This closed in July 1980 and was demolished in 1982. In 1929 the Plaza, later the Odeon came. This opened at 125-7 The Parade, High Street on the corner of Albert Road. At the time, with seating for 2,060, it was the largest cinema in Hertfordshire. It survived until November 1963. The site is now occupied by Destiny nightclub.

The Gaumont, also later to become an Odeon, opened at 65 The Parade in the High Street in May 1937. In October 1983 it closed and was demolished. In 1937 another Odeon opened at 405 St Albans Road, North Watford, closing in May 1959. It was demolished, and following a transformation into a Waitrose Supermarket, it went the way of much suburban land and a block of flats was built on the site.[4]

THEATRES

Building of the Palace Theatre in Clarendon Road began in 1908 and it was completed in 1910. The architect was W A Theobold and the stone front was added by Wylson and Long in 1909-10. For a while music hall acts alternated with plays and early films and from the beginning touring companies visited. In the 1930s weekly repertory was established and this continued during and after the war. By 1965 the theatre was in financial difficulties and with the backing of Watford Council a Civic Theatre Trust took over the building, after which the theatre became one of the best known venues outside London. In April 2002 the theatre was awarded £5 million from the National Lottery so as to renovate the building, the theatre organisers raising over £2 million themselves. It has since been refurbished while retaining much of its original lively interior.

134. An early theatre in Watford is noted in this advertisement from The Times *of 5 July, 1790.*

BY DESIRE OF

Mr. and Mrs. B U X T O N,

The laſt N I G H T.

Mr. J O N E S's B E N E F I T

TUESDAY June 4, at Watford new Theatre, Will be held up to view, the Mirror of Nature; JONES takes for his Benefit,

135. *The Palace Theatre in Clarendon Road.*

1   Cussans, John Edwin, *History of Hertfordshire* Vol. 3 p165 (1881)

2   Philips, Oliver, *The official centenary hihstory of Watford FC 1881-1991.* I am indebted to this volume for the section on Watford Football Club.

3   I am very grateful to Sarah Priestley, Heritage Officer at the Watford Museum, for her input and help with this section.

4   Eyles, Allen and Skone, Keith, *Cinemas of Hertfordshire* (2002)

Wartimes

THE BOER WAR 1899-1902

A volunteer company of the Herts Yeomanry trained in Cassiobury Park prior to serving in South Africa. On 3 March 1900 the company marched out of the town via the Market Square to Watford Junction Station where they embarked for Tilbury. They were led by Captain Gilliat, and his second in command, the Earl of Essex.

In this war seven of the company were killed and 35 wounded.

THE GREAT WAR 1914-1918

The First World War or Great War as it was then known, left few if any communities untouched: Watford suffered appalling losses. The Hertfordshire Yeomanry was mobilised in August 1914 and saw service in Egypt, Gallipoli and the Middle East, and some units ended the war in India. There was initial

patriotic pride and a desire to take part and do one's duty, but there was later disillusionment when the losses began to affect large numbers of Watford families. One eye witness tells us that on the declaration of war there was

"from the very outset, the excitement, the stir, and the gravity of mobilisation... the continuous procession of troops, on foot and mounted through the town on the Saturday and Sunday, August 8 and 9; the departure of the Herts Territorials; the 'Good-bye' and the 'Good luck' of parents to sons; those comfortable sleek horses hitched to transport wagons just commandeered from the happy harvest fields – are the lasting local memories of those who remembered the first week of the war."

The Herts Territorials had bestowed on them a signal honour: they were among the first of the territorial regiments to fight in Belgium. "You'll find it a warm corner", they were told on taking up their position in the firing line, November 1914. The "warm corner" was a

136. Hertfordshire Yeomanry on parade in the High Street c. 1890, with the Essex Arms Hotel in the background.

137. 1st World War soldiers marching past the pond at the northern end of the High Street.

section of the line between Ypres and the Belgian coast, and the Herts Territorials took a share in the saving of Calais and the Channel ports from the Germans. Our eye-witness then goes on to describe the visible effects on Watford as the war progressed:

"...and when the conflict deepened and the withdrawal of so many men began to be felt in the general life of the community, the towns folk rose to the occasion. We became familiar with the sight of post-women; of women delivering bread or milk; voluntary helpers assisted in the working of the District Hospital; the call for special police met with a splendid response; a Volunteer Training Corps sprang into being. St John Ambulance men turned out when enemy air-raids were expected [though Watford escaped attacks]. A Zeppelin passed over the north-west of the town; an enemy plane hummed overhead one moonlight night; and on 23 occasions the town was in darkness because of expected air-raids."

The many who did not return from overseas are recorded in the town Roll of Honour held by the Central Library.[1]

138. A sad reminder of the human toll of the Great War. The grave of Private G W Hawkins, died January 1917 aged 27. One of a number of that war's graves in the Vicarage Road cemetery.

139. The Peace Memorial which originally stood outside the Peace Memorial Hospital, but is now outside the Town Hall. It commemorates the wounded and dead from both world wars.

140. The inscription on the memorial.

Heroes the men might have been, but another reminiscence of a resident of this period illustrates the grim reality of post-war Watford.

"...sometimes little groups of be-medalled ex-Servicemen from the First World War would appear in the streets singing or playing musical instruments in the hope that they could earn a little money. These ex-Service veterans had been promised a brave new world on the cessation of hostilities, but were not able to be found employment, were given no pensions and no scheme such as the dole was in force. They were therefore obliged to beg in the streets to obtain money."[2]

There were two munitions factories in Watford, one on Imperial Way and one at Greycaines. These produced mortar bombs, grenades, smoke canisters and small arms magazines.

One of the benefits to Watford of the war was the founding of the Peace Memorial Hospital which opened in June 1928.

The War Memorial in Watford Cemetery in Vicarage Road was erected under the instructions of the Imperial War Graves Commission in 1929. It was dedicated to "the memory of members of His Majesty's Forces who gave their lives for the country in the Great War, 1914-1918, and who lie buried in the Borough of Watford". The Memorial is to the left as one walks into the cemetery.

THE SECOND WORLD WAR

War against Germany was declared on 3 September 1939, but Watford, like many towns, had been preparing for it since 1938. Large scale military exercises were held during 1938, and Watford had two anti-aircraft batteries in place. Communal air-raid shelters were set up in Cassiobury Park on the corner of St Albans Road and Balmoral Road and Albert Road North.

The Local Defence Force – the Home Guard – was formed in 1940. Watford had four battalions, but it was the 6th Battalion which specifically covered Watford.

Many local factories were turned over to war production. Sun Engraving produced maps and aerial photographs of occupied Europe. These were used in the D-day landings in June 1944. Sun also produced parts for bulldozers, tanks, Bren gun carriers and anti-aircraft shells.

61 citizens of Watford were killed and 121 injured during the conflict. The worst incident was the V1 flying-bomb which fell on Sandringham Road, North Watford on 31 July 1944, killing 40 people. The immediacy of this tragedy is brought to us by two accounts. Mrs. Dorrice Ephithite recalls:

"I occupied a back bedroom with my husband at 101 Sandringham Road. In the front bedroom were my daughter, son-in-law and their little girl. The sirens sounded about 12 midnight and I got up and got dressed and then went back and lay on the bed. About 3 o'clock in the morning, the house was struck by a flying bomb... I was covered in debris and my husband was beside me... Men came in the dark and got me out... I was among the bricks at the back of the house... I was taken to Parkgate School and I did not see or hear anything of my daughter."

141. *Watford Junction station in 1939. Children being evacuated.*

142. Watford Home Guard Victory march-past in 1945.

Mrs Ephithite's husband, daughter, son-in-law and 2½-year-old granddaughter were killed, and are buried with some of the other victims in a special grave at North Watford Cemetery. A rescuer from the Watford District Rescue Service described the aftermath of the explosion:

"I started digging, we found the body of a woman in night attire in the front of the house... the body was handed over to colleagues... We found the body of a man beside the previous one."[3]

The final toll for Watford was 58 houses totally destroyed, 261 seriously damaged, and 2,400 with minor damage.

PEACE AGAIN

In April 1945 Watford Borough Council issued a programme to celebrate VE Day. This included an interdenominational Thanksgiving Service at the Town Hall. On the day itself the High Street was decked in a sea of red, white and blue, and in contrast to the long blackout endured during the war, the Council lit up every possible building, and fairy lights were strung along the walks in Cassiobury Park. In excess of 10,000 people celebrated in the park and there were bonfires in the High Street and Water Lane. An attempt by the Fire Brigade to extinguish these fires failed when the crowds refused to allow them access.

1   Saunders, *History of Watford* p59
2   From J. Gloag's 'Reminiscences of Watford', available in the Watford Central Library reference section
3   Information Watford Museum

Watford Museum

Watford Museum, the home of much of the town's heritage, is itself within an historic house. The building is a mansion of 1775 and was purchased in 1867 by Joseph Benskin of the brewery company. He lived there until his death in 1877.

The house adjoined the brewery and was described in 1891 in *Noted Brewers of Great Britain and Ireland* as follows: "On the right of the gateway stands an ancient mansion, the residence of former proprietors, and now occupied by the widow of the late Mr Benskin. It is a beautiful old place with its background of flower gardens, lawns and stately trees, and presents a pleasant picture of ancient well-to-do country life." In 1975 Watford bought the site and in 1981 the house was opened as Watford's museum.

THE ART COLLECTION

Watford has in its museum a splendid collection of portraits of the Essex families which span over two centuries. The oldest and among the finest is that of Robert Devereux (1566-1601), 2nd Earl of Essex, Queen Elizabeth I's favourite during the later years of her life. He was not connected with the Cassiobury Earls of Essex although, coincidentally, in 1645 his son the 3rd Earl (1591-1646) was granted Lord Capel's Watford estates for services to the Parliamentary cause. At the Restoration Capel's son was restored to these and, ironically, bestowed with the then defunct title of Earl of Essex. The culminating portrait is of George Capel Coningsby, 5th Earl of the 7th creation, who was himself a great patron of the arts during the first quarter of the 19th century.

These paintings represent a cross-section of the changing image of the English face – albeit only from the upper echelons of society – as depicted by some of the most outstanding itinerant portrait painters, largely foreign, working in England between 1590 and 1830, when the art form was at its zenith.

Chronologically the collection begins with Marcus Gheeraerts' studio portrait of Robert Devereux, which exemplifies brilliantly late

143. The Watford Museum building when part of the Benskin's Brewery.

144. The Watford Museum in 2005.

16th-century Elizabethan painting. From the following century come Sir Peter Lely's depictions of Arthur Capel and Elizabeth Percy, the 1st Earl and Countess of Essex. They represent the era of the great state portraiture, echoing the grandeur of Sir Anthony van Dyck. The Lelys are followed by the more sober, new generation portraits produced at the end of the 17th century, exemplified in the collection by the works of Sir Godfrey Kneller.

Sir Joshua Reynolds, among the greatest exponents of the Romantic era who took the genre to a new level of importance, is represented by the delightful portrait of Frances Hanbury Williams, wife of William Anne Holles, 4th Earl of Essex. The portrait shows a greater degree of self-awareness hitherto not seen in the English portrait painting. Sir Thomas Lawrence's studio portrait of the 5th Earl of Essex represents a return to the type of state portraits showing a concern for the superficial appearance of the sitter.

There are likewise excellent examples of lesser-known artists who are, only now, being recognised for their talent – among them William Wissing, who came from the Netherlands to work for Lely, and Enoch Seeman, who painted for the Royal Family during the first half of the 18th century.

This section is based upon information supplied by Dr. Laurie Harwood and Watford Museum. The Museum offers a range of services for groups and societies including a High Street trail. Members of the museum team are available to give talks on the history of Cassiobury or Watford's High Street.

For more information contact Watford Museum at 194 Watford High Street, Herts, WD17 2DT. (Telephone: 01923 232297 or email info@watfordmuseum.org.uk.)

Opening times are Thursday–Saturday, 10am-5pm. Admission is free.

Further Reading

Of early vintage is Sir Henry Chauncy's magnificently titled *The Historical Antiquities of Hertfordshire, with the Original of Counties, Hundreds or Wapentakes and Hamlets; the Foundation and Origin of Monasteries, Churches, and Vicarages; the Several Honors, Mannors, and Parks of the Nobility and Gentry; and the Succession of the Lords Each. Faithfully collected from Public Records, Ancient Manuscripts and Other Select Authorities* (1700). This book is available in the reference section of the Watford Central Library.

Watford's proximity to London and St Albans has ensured that from the time of Domesday not only have records survived but Watford has been of interest to many who have lived there, such as Robert Clutterbuck, or those who just passed through. Clutterbuck, a member of a prominent local family wrote *The History and Antiquities of the County of Hertford*. The first volume deals with Watford (1815), and is available at the Rickmansworth Library.

John Britton, writing in the early 19th century, produced two relevant works, in 1810 *The Beauties of England and Wales*, and in 1837 *The History and Description, with Graphic Illustrations, of Cassiobury Park, Hertfordshire, the Seat of the Earl of Essex*. Both works are rich in illustrations and are available at the Watford Central Library, reference section.

John Cussans wrote a *History of Hertfordshire*, which was publsihed in 1881. This is available in the Watford Central Library, reference section.

There are a number of less formal recollections and histories which provide an insight into life in Watford during the 19th century. Probably the best of these is by Henry Williams, born 1828 in Watford, who lived in Queens Road (died 1893). He wrote a *History of Watford* in 1883., restricted to 1000 copies. The work is of particular interest in that much of it comprises conversation with locals, and information obtained from gossip and rumour. The style is light and interesting and deals with the everyday cares and concerns of local residents.

Bibliography

Ball, Alan William, and Watford Council: *Street and Place Names in Watford*. Watford Borough Council (1973).

Britton, John: *The History and Description, with Graphic Illustrations of Cassiobury Park, Hertfordshire: The Seat of the Earl of Essex*. Published by the Author, Burton Street, London (1837).

Britton, John and Evans, John, *The Beauties of England and Wales: Or Delineations Topographical, Historical and Descriptive of Each County etc,*. London, Verner, Hood & Sharpe (1810).

Castle, Stephen A: *Timber-Framed Buildings in Watford*. Occasional Paper published by Phillimore for the Hertfordshire Local History Council (1977).

Chauncy, Sir Henry: *The Historical Antiquities of Hertfordshire. With the Original of Counties, Hundreds or Wapentakes and Hamlets; the Foundation and Origin of Monasteries, Churches, and Vicarages; the Several Honors, Mannors, and Parks of the Nobility and Gentry; and the Succession of the Lords Each. Faithfully Collected from Public Records, Ancient Manuscripts and Other Select Authorities*. London, B. Griffin, S. Keble (1700).

Clutterbuck, Robert: T*he History and Antiquities of the County of Hertford etc*. Vol. 1; London, Nichols, son, and Bentley (1815).

A Complete History and development of All the Extraordinary Circumstances and Events Connected with the Murder of Mr. Weare: Together with the Trial at Large: Including the Speeches of Counsel-Examination of Evidence-Defence. The Whole forming a Genuine Series of Gambling Biography. London, Jones & Co., (1824).

Conder, Eustace R, and Conder, Josiah: *A Memoir*, London J. Snow (1857).

Connell, Nicholas, and Stratton, Ruth, *Hertfordshire Murders,* Sutton (2003).

Cussans, John Edwin, *History of Hertfordshire: Containing an Account of the Descents of the Various Manors; Pedigrees of Families connected with the County: Antiquities, Local Customs, &C., &Co. Chiefly compiled from Original Mss. In the Record Office and British Museum, Parochial Registers, Local Archives, and Collections in Possession of Private Families.* 3 vols. London, Chatto & Windus (1881).

Defoe, Daniel, and Richardson, Samuel: *A Tour through the Island of Great Britain.* W Strahan *(et al)* (1778).

Eyles, Allen, and Skone, Keith: *Cinemas of Hertfordshire.* New edition, Hertfordshire Publications (2002).

Faulkner, Alan H: *The George & the Mary: A Brief History of the Grand Union Canal Carrying Company Ltd,* published by Robert Wilson, 38 Greenhill Road, Kettering (1973)

Groves, Tim, *et al, From the Wheatsheaf to the Windmill: The story of Bushey and Oxhey pubs.* Bushey Museum Trust (1984).

Knight, Judith and Flood, Susan: *Two Nineteenth Century Hertfordshire Diaries.* Hertfordshire Record Society (2002).

Lewis, Samuel: *Topographical Dictionary of England.* 4 vols, London (1831).

Nunn, J B, *The Book of Watford* 1 & 2 (1996)

Old Inhabitant and County of Hertford. A Guide to Hertfordshire, with a History and Description of the Various Towns and Villages. Hertford (1880).

Osborn, Neil: 'The Story of Hertfordshire Police' in *Hertfordshire Countryside* (1969).

Victoria County History of Hertfordshire, vol. 2 (1902).

Phillips, Oliver: *The Official Centenary History of Watford FC*

Salmon, N: *The History of Hertfordshire.* London (1728).

Saunders, William, R., *History of Watford* (1931) reprint edition with new foreword 1970

Stratton, Ruth and Connell, Nicholas: *Haunted Hertfordshire: A Ghostly Gazetteer.* Book Castle (2003).

Thomas, William Beach, *Hertfordshire,* (1950)

Tomkins, Malcolm and Javes, Graham: *So that was Hertfordshire: Travellers' Jottings 1322-1887,* Hertfordshire Publications (1998).

Toynbee Paget Jackson and Toynbee, Helen: *The Letters of Horace Walpole, Fourth Earl of Orford. Chronologically arranged and edited with notes and indices by Mrs Paget Toynbee.* (1903).

Williams, Henry: *History of Watford, and Trade Directory.* Pardon & Sons (1884).

Watford WEA, *Aspects of Nineteenth Century Watford.*

Index

An asterisk denotes an illustration or caption